The Lord's Prayer

Alan Gonzalez

For information write:
The Salvation Army
USA Southern Territory
Literary Council
1424 Northeast Expressway
Atlanta, GA 30329

ISBN: 978-0-86544-069-2

Editors: Linda & Lynell Johnson, The WordWorking Shop
Cover Art: Erin Wyatt
Printed in the United States of America

Dedication:

For all those who seek, try,
or wish to approach God
with all their heart and
want to pray differently.

Table of Contents

Introduction

WHILE I WAS LEADING A small congregation in Georgia, we started a program of home Bible studies. I was moved to teach about the Lord's Prayer. It is a prayer that most of us have been familiar with since childhood. We learned to repeat it often, perhaps from memory. But for many of us, it has no more special meaning than any other formal invocation or religious formula.

Yet the Lord's Prayer—which is really a *pattern* for prayer that Jesus gave to His disciples—contains the foundation for building a strong, intimate relationship with God. When we consider each word carefully, we come to understand who God is and how He wants us to see Him, as our Father. We also learn how very much He cares about our total well–being—body, soul, and spirit.

I decided to write this book as a series of reflections on the Lord's Prayer for those who have had little connection with the prayer as well as for those who know the words by heart. Its purpose is to explore in depth Jesus' intention behind this teaching.

My prayer is that whoever reads this book will be inspired by it. I am convinced that anyone who undertakes a careful study of the Lord's Prayer will be rewarded with a clearer perception of God, a transformed prayer life, and an increase in the perfecting of their faith.

Alan J. Gonzalez

The Prayer

Therefore pray in this manner:

Our Father who is in heaven,
hallowed be Your name.

Your kingdom come;
Your will be done
on earth, as it is in heaven.

Give us this day our daily bread.

And forgive us our debts,
as we forgive our debtors.

And lead us not into temptation,
but deliver us from evil.

For Yours is the kingdom
and the power
and the glory forever.

Amen

Matthew 6:9–13

1

"Lord, teach us to pray"

Seek God with all your heart

A COOL BREEZE FROM THE Sea of Galilee was caressing the shores of Capernaum that morning. The sun was just beginning to shine, and fishing boats could be seen coming in to land after a long night in deep waters. The 12 men who were closest to Jesus wondered what had happened to Him. They puzzled over where the Master had spent the night, as the sleeping place they had prepared for Him was untouched. Then one of them noticed a man coming down the nearby mountain; when the man neared the village, they realized that it was Jesus.

All that night the Lord had been praying. Alone, away from the hustle and bustle of the crowd that came to hear Him and to be healed, the Son of God had spent the hours of darkness in the presence of His heavenly Father. His face reflected a deep peace and serenity that seemed to spread among those who approached Him.

One of Jesus' disciples, knowing what He had been doing during the night, said to Him, *"Lord, teach us to pray."*

How long the Master had awaited that request! Since the time the Lord called these Twelve and they made the decision to follow Him, many extraordinary things had happened. The disciples had listened as Jesus taught the people the truths of God's kingdom. They had seen Him perform great signs and wonders, one after another. However, with all that they had seen, and as much as they had learned from the Master, they were not satisfied. Suddenly, they understood that the source of Jesus' continuing power was the time He spent in prayer. They realized that they too needed to pray and they wanted to do it as Jesus did, but they didn't know how.

Jesus knew exactly how to pray; He had plenty of experience to draw on.

I always wondered why Jesus prayed so much. From my first steps as a Christian, I learned (and I believe) that Jesus Christ is one Person of the Trinity, who preexisted Creation. In fact, He made all things. (John 1:3) In Him *"lives all the fullness of God in a human body."* (Colossians 2:9 *NLT*) Yet He prayed.

One day, while driving to the office, I suddenly felt that the Holy Spirit had given me the answer. At that moment I understood that the prayer life of Jesus is a powerful witness to His perfect humanity. The Bible says that He *"emptied himself, taking the form of a slave, being born in human likeness."* (Philippians 2:7 *NRSV*) As a human being, Jesus not only desired to pray, to spend time with His Father, but He also needed to pray in order to receive divine guidance and power.

Jesus prayed, and His Father always listened to Him. (John 11:42) Unclean spirits obeyed His orders, the sick were healed, the dead were raised, and the teachers of the Law could not resist His wisdom. And Jesus' desire is that the Father will also listen to us. He came to make us one with the Father, and prayer is part of the plan.

Jesus presents to us a perfect model of voluntary obedience. He assumed the attitude of the creature before the Creator: humility and dependence. In a world that wanted independence from God, Jesus remained submissive, subject to the will of the Father. The *"Wonderful Counselor, Mighty God"* of whom Isaiah prophesied (Isaiah 9:6) displayed a meek and humble heart. He knew how to pray.

Communion with God

The small group of men gathered on Galilee's shore that day were not novices, just beginning to be interested in spiritual disciplines. It's likely that before meeting with Jesus, they all had been regular members of the local synagogue and faithful believers in the official religion.

As Jews, they had been subject since childhood to a religious system that governed virtually all facets of their lives: they had been circumcised on the eighth day as commanded by the Law of Moses (much of which they had memorized); they celebrated holy days, offered sacrifices, and abstained from forbidden foods—just as their parents, grandparents, and ancestors had done. But then, suddenly, Jesus appeared to each of them in the middle of their daily occupations and called them, without explanation, to follow Him. And they left everything to do just that. They could not resist His call.

Jesus' message represented something new, a way of looking at things that was radically different from the religious and social environment the disciples had known until then. Many of Jesus' teachings were mysterious to them, and some seemed unduly harsh. Gradually, each of these disciples came to believe that Jesus was actually "the hope of Israel," the Messiah they had been awaiting for so long. When others turned away from Him, Jesus asked the Twelve, *"Do you also wish to go away?"* Peter spoke on behalf of the group when he said, *"Lord, to whom can we go? You have the words of eternal life."* (John 6:67–68 *NRSV*)

The request the unnamed disciple made to Jesus was: *"Lord, teach us to pray, just as John taught his disciples."* (Luke 11:1) The Bible offers no indication of the instructions given by John the Baptizer to his disciples concerning prayer. It's possible that his prayers followed an Old Testament pattern. At best, John's knowledge of God's heavenly plan was imperfect; Jesus, who lived in intimate communion with His Father, knew it in detail.

So the very Son of God revealed with authority the most appropriate way to pray. "Teach us to pray" means "Teach us to talk to God in such a way that we will be heard. Reveal to us the secret of asking, of interceding for others and expressing our own needs to Him so that we can be sure He listens to us."

Prayer, maintaining contact and communion with God, is the essential means for any believer by which to keep from falling. John Bunyan said, "Prayer will make a man cease from sin, or sin will entice a man to cease from prayer."[1] Eve stopped communicating openly with God to exchange arguments with the deceiver instead; as a result, she and Adam became separated from the Creator. Jesus, the "second Adam" (1 Corinthians 15:45), knew that He, and all those who would follow Him, needed to stay in unceasing contact with the One who is above everything and everyone.

---

1   "John Bunyan's Dying Sayings" in Offor's 1861 edition of *Bunyan's Works*.

Commitment to prayer

Among all the definitions of prayer that have been suggested, the most common is: "Prayer is talking to God." That sounds simple; however, in practice, prayer is a discipline, and every discipline has rules and demands effort. I offer this explanation by way of definition:

> *Prayer is a testimony of dependence and an act of surrender to a Being who is infinitely greater than ourselves. It is a way of exalting that Being and recognizing His nature, His attributes, and His ability to meet all our needs; a way to sustain our hope, dispel our fears, and reaffirm, while living in this world, the values on which our faith is founded.*

The subject of prayer is of great importance to every Christian. It is emphasized throughout the Bible. These exhortations come from our Lord Himself:

- *"Jesus told his disciples a parable to show them that they should always pray and not give up."* (Luke 18:1)

- *" 'Watch and pray so that you will not fall into temptation.' "* (Matthew 26:41)

- *" 'Pray for those who persecute you.' "* (Matthew 5:44)

From the Apostle Paul:
- *"Pray in the Spirit on all occasions with all kinds of prayers and requests."* (Ephesians 6:18)

- *"Devote yourselves to prayer, being watchful and thankful."* (Colossians 4:2)

- *"Pray without ceasing."* (1 Thessalonians 5:17 *NRSV)*

And from James:

- *"Pray for each other so that you may be healed. The prayer of a righteous person is powerful and effective."* (James 5:16)

The Apostle Peter writes that Jesus left an example, *"that you should follow in his steps"* (1 Peter 2:21). Jesus prayed all the time; so should we. There can be no consecrated life or spiritual development without the practice of prayer—Jesus' way.

What about you?

What about you? What is your religious experience? Perhaps you are a person committed to your faith; maybe it is only a matter of tradition, or what you learned at home. Perhaps you are indifferent or neutral, although you pray occasionally. Why do you pray? How do you pray? The question should be: Do you pray according to the will of God?

Have you ever purchased one of those devices that come "Assembly Required"? I remember once when we bought a set of equipment for the church to use for simultaneous translation, English to Spanish, in the worship services. I was happy about the new acquisition, and on Sunday morning I installed all the components. However, my excitement didn't last long, because the system didn't work. Everything seemed to be connected properly, with the batteries in place … but no sound. I checked the brief instructions accompanying the equipment, which I had followed during installation, and reviewed them one by one. Finally, I found this advice: "IF ALL THE ABOVE DOES NOT WORK SEE THE MANUFACTURER'S MANUAL AND READ THE

INSTRUCTIONS AGAIN." I did, and I succeeded; what hadn't been working now worked.

How is your prayer life? Perhaps it is routine, inconsistent, empty, or even nonexistent. Maybe you have come to feel that prayer is not worth wasting your time on if you never get the answer you expect. Or maybe you pray on a regular basis, but it has become rote, with no real connection to the Father. Or perhaps you believe in the value and power of prayer, but you're not satisfied and want to go deeper. In any case, at heart you know there is something wrong. Why not turn to the "Manufacturer's Manual" AND READ THE INSTRUCTIONS AGAIN? Look to *"Jesus, the author and finisher of our faith"* (Hebrews 12:2 *NKJV*) to learn how to pray. The most successful and effective disciples in Christian history have understood this; they may have tried various methods, beliefs, or styles, but they found out their system didn't work.

What you know about prayer won't do you any good unless you actually pray according to the model our Master has provided. The Lord's Prayer is the Manufacturer's Manual, with the "assembly instructions" for the system that guarantees direct, effective communication with our heavenly Father. God is waiting for you. He says: *"You will seek me and find me when you seek me with all your heart."* (Jeremiah 29:13) He wants to *"show you great and mighty things, which you do not know."* (Jeremiah 33:3 *NKJV*)

The Apostle John said that *"if we ask anything according to [God's] will, he hears us."* (1 John 5:14) Is it your desire to pray and be heard by God, and do it according to His will? Not just as a pious act of repetitive words, but as an expression of dependence and submission to the Almighty? Prayer isn't just about seeking solutions to our problems; it is also the way to have fellowship with God. Prayer brings us closer to Him, and through it our spirit is strengthened and our soul becomes sensitive to His voice.

When you pray as Jesus taught, your voice will be projected into the very presence of God, crossing the heavens, challenging circumstances, overcoming obstacles, grasping the hem of His garment, from which springs miraculous power. (Luke 8:43–48)

I think that by the evening of that day in Galilee a new era had begun for that group of disciples. They would learn by experience that this teaching was for every day of their lives. This teaching was necessary if they wanted to avoid falling into temptation, to testify, to receive God's power; it would be necessary as they faced the challenge to persevere in worship despite flogging and persecution. Ultimately, these men would find in prayer the strength to shake the foundations of one of the most rigid empires in history. And only eternity will reveal the impact that the request of that disciple and Jesus' response has had on the lives of millions of believers all over the world.

It is my prayer that, by God's grace and with the help of the Holy Spirit, this book will help you learn to pray, and to pray more effectively. Each phrase of the Lord's Prayer conveys lessons that bear on our relationship with God, the meeting of our needs, and dealing with our neighbor.

Let us pray …

Heavenly Father, first I want to thank you because
I can pray. To be able to approach you is a privilege
of which I am not worthy. I can do so only through
Jesus Christ, but because of Him, I am confident
that you will listen to me. Father, just as the disciples
approached Jesus eager to learn how to pray, so do I
come to you. Teach me to make prayer my priority in
all the circumstances of life. Give me wisdom to pray
according to your will, so that I will know not only
that you hear me, but also that you will answer me.

Amen

2

"Our Father ... "

Exercise your privileges as God's child

TWO YEARS AFTER MARY AND I were married, Alan Jr. was born, adding a new dimension to our lives. From that moment, we committed to responsibly serving this helpless creature God had placed in our care; that included feeding him properly, protecting him—in short, loving him. As a parent, I took on the task of helping my son walk the path through childhood and adolescence until he reached maturity.

One of the most celebrated events for us was when our son first said the word "dad" (at least, that's what we heard). I was filled with emotion; it was the highlight of my week. We would immediately tell everyone who visited us that our child had called me "Dad."

I associate my experience with what I believe God Himself must feel when we call Him "Dad." But we need to do this with an awareness of what it means to call God our Father.

The object of our prayers

The first instruction in the Manufacturer's Manual concerning prayer is this: those who pray must pray only to God. Jesus does

NOT give instructions at any time about praying to angels, saints, or anyone or anything other than God Himself. Such devotion, whether in praise or in confession of need, belongs only to Him, the source and sustainer of all creation.

"In the beginning God created the heavens and the earth." (Genesis 1:1) In the majestic environment of His celestial projects office, God put together, in detail and with divine creativity, the design of the things we see and enjoy, the cosmos in its entirety.

> 'To whom will you compare me? Or who is my equal?'
> says the Holy One. Lift up your eyes and look to the
> heavens: Who created all these? He who brings out the
> starry host one by one and calls forth each of them by
> name. Because of his great power and mighty strength,
> not one of them is missing. (Isaiah 40:25–26)

I imagine young David was entertained watching the starry sky above the Bethlehem region while tending his father's sheep, especially on clear nights, when the constellations were more clearly visible and meteors left trails of blazing light. To David the poet, everything he saw had a meaning beyond the obvious. The size, the color, the brightness, the twinkling of each star was something unique. Perhaps those memories were in David's mind when he wrote: "The heavens declare the glory of God; the skies proclaim the work of his hands." (Psalm 19:1)

God is also the sustainer, who assumes direct, ongoing responsibility for His creation. The philosophy of deism holds that God put the world into motion, like a clock, and then just let it run, with no further activity on His part. Such a conception of God is profoundly contrary to the nature of His person and attributes. He does not ignore His creation. He is especially concerned about all living creatures. Jesus taught that God feeds the birds of the air and clothes the grass of the field—and that He cares far more about the life of every human being. (Matthew 6:26, 28–30)

The Apostle Paul wrote, *"I kneel before the Father, from whom every family in heaven and on earth derives its name."* (Ephesians 3:14–15) In a sense, every human being carries the "name" of God. His seal is in our genes, because what gives life to those genes is the breath of God.

The culture of God's kingdom

"Our Father ... " These words must have had a terrific impact on the disciples. Each of us is born into a particular cultural context and, inevitably, we are marked socially, psychologically, and spiritually by the set of beliefs, customs, and other elements that make up this culture.

Let's place ourselves for a moment in the shoes of any Jew of Jesus' time. Let's imagine being there when Jesus began His teaching about prayer. We wait for the first words out of His mouth, and we hear Him say, *"Therefore pray in this manner: Our Father ... "* Given our Jewish culture, we would likely think: *Wait a minute! We're not used to praying that way. Moses didn't pray that way. Neither did Samuel, David, Elijah—not even the prophet Isaiah.*

Every Jewish male had to study, from childhood, the books of Moses: Genesis, Exodus, Leviticus, Numbers, and Deuteronomy. According to those books, God's revelation of Himself was accompanied by great and awesome displays of power. Moses' first encounter with God came on a mountainside in the Sinai Desert, when God called to him out of a burning bush and gave him the impossible assignment of liberating the Israelites from slavery in Egypt. What followed was a series of amazing, wonderful—and sometimes very frightening—miracles by which God displayed His love for His people and His anger against the Pharaoh, the king of Egypt, and many others who opposed them. In the books of Moses, the *Lord* is presented as an almighty sovereign to whom all should be submissive, one who rewards obedience but severely punishes disobedience.

Under the Law of Moses, the priest played a decisive role in a relationship with God. He was the intermediary, the bridge connecting the creature with the Creator. In the Old Testament, there were some instances in which God dealt with an individual one–on–one, but that was not the norm. So in the collective Jewish mind, a direct, personal relationship with the Father was practically inconceivable.

Yet God repeatedly expressed an unmatched tenderness toward His people, the Israelites. This grew out of the intimate relationship between God and Abraham. God called the nation of Israel, Abraham's descendants, *"my firstborn son"* (Exodus 4:22). Even when the Israelites were unfaithful to their covenant with God—and suffered the consequences—God remained faithful and did not abandon them.

There were times when it seemed that God had forgotten His people. But He gave them a message that reflected His commitment to the nation He loved: *"Can a mother forget the baby at her breast and have no compassion for the child she has borne? Though she may forget, I will not forget you!"* (Isaiah 49:15)

Still, what Jesus taught about prayer, like much of His teaching, differed radically from the cultural expectations of His hearers. The image of God that He presented was not that of a faraway, fearsome being whom only a chosen few could approach. In the Tabernacle—later the Temple—of Israel, a heavy curtain cut off the Most Holy Place where God dwelt. Only a high priest could enter there.

Jesus came to change all that, to tear away the curtain, to open "a new and living way" into the presence of God (Hebrews 10:20), offering free, unhindered access of the kind a child would have in approaching her or his father. We are encouraged to *"approach God's throne of grace with confidence, so that we may receive mercy and find grace to help us in our time of need."* (Hebrews 4:16) In the culture of God's kingdom, the emphasis is not on the authoritarian God who *"is a consuming fire"* (Deuteronomy 4:24) so much as it is on the compassionate God who *"is love"* (1 John 4:16).

The character of our Father

Jesus teaches us that communion with God is based on a relationship of trust and intimacy. We reach the status of God's "children" by an act of His grace, which is then sealed through regeneration by the Holy Spirit. Everything God does for us as His children is the result of His love.

In considering our personal relationship with the Father, it's important to recognize the nature of His character.

- God is absolutely faithful.
- God is absolutely just.
- God is absolutely good.
- God is absolutely true.

Whenever we pray, we must believe that our Father is able to satisfy all our material, emotional, and spiritual needs, as promised in His Word: *"My God will meet all your needs according to the riches of his glory in Christ Jesus."* (Philippians 4:19) After all, *"What is impossible for mere humans is possible for God."* (Luke 18:27 *NET)* When God receives us as children, He takes responsibility for looking after us and providing for us for the present and for the future. He uses His unlimited power for our well–being.

However, we must remember that God is also a righteous Father who acts according to His good and perfect will. He will not deny us anything that is good for us. So if what we ask for is necessary and good, we can ask with confidence. God is more understanding than the most accommodating of human parents.

Further, we should not think of God only as a providing Father. He exercises all the functions that would be expected of a father who loves his children. Due to the interest that our Heavenly Father has in perfecting our character and our relationship with Him, He will correct us when He deems it necessary.

'My child, don't make light of the Lord's discipline,
and don't give up when he corrects you.
For the Lord disciplines those he loves,
and he punishes each one he accepts as his child.'

As you endure this divine discipline, remember that God is treating you as his own children. Who ever heard of a child who is never disciplined by its father? If God doesn't discipline you as he does all of his children, it means that you are illegitimate and not really his children at all. (Hebrews 12:5–8 NLT)

God also seeks to teach us to have moral judgment, to understand the difference between right and wrong. Through His Word and by His Spirit, our Father tells us exactly what to do and what to avoid. These constraints on our behavior are imposed in order that we might please Him, and to protect us from the consequences of wrong behavior.

Analyzing the implications of all these truths, we see that when we call God "Father," we assume a very large commitment. We are not only to believe in Him, but also to strive to be like Him. Paul exhorts us: *"Therefore be imitators of God, as beloved children."* (Ephesians 5:1 *NRSV)* Our responsibility is to become like our Father in His holiness, love, and willingness to forgive.

What about you?

What is your conception of the God to whom you pray? Do you think of Him as a distant Being who doesn't care about you and your problems? Do you see Him as a tyrant who must be obeyed in order to obtain some favor from Him? Perhaps, since childhood, you have often heard it said: "If you misbehave, God will punish you." Thus, your image of Him is that of a severe, angry God.

Jesus teaches us another, better way of relating to God. He offers us a new image, the paternal face of a God who wants to be near His children. Our Father wants to show us the width and length and height and depth of His great love.

Perhaps, like most Christians, you learned to pray the Lord's Prayer at an early age, but it never had much meaning for you. What will you do now that you know that God loves you as the Father whose interest in you is perfect and eternal?

Let us pray ...

Almighty God, I bless you because I can call you
my Father. Thank you that in your eyes, I am not
just a creature, but your child. I know that you take
responsibility for me and that I am under your care.
I know that you will not allow me to lack anything
that is good for me. Father, I promise to respect you,
to honor you, and to live a life worthy of a child of
yours.

Amen

3

"Who is in heaven ... "

Recognize the greatness of God

JESUS CALLED HEAVEN *"MY FATHER'S house"* (John 14:2). Heaven is the center of power where the government of the universe resides.

When Moses built the Tabernacle in the wilderness, God promised to manifest Himself within the Most Holy Place, where the Ark of the Covenant was located. But He wanted to make clear from whence He spoke to His people: *"Then the Lord said to Moses: 'Tell the Israelites this: "You have seen for yourselves that I have spoken to you from heaven." ' "* (Exodus 20:22)

In place of the Tabernacle, King Solomon built a Temple in Jerusalem. On opening day, God promised that His Name, His eyes, and His heart would dwell there and that He would listen to prayers offered in that place. (2 Chronicles 7:12, 15–16)

At the time Jesus was teaching His disciples about prayer, all Jews were convinced that God still dwelt in the Temple and that that was the place where He should be worshiped. However, Jerusalem was under pagan Roman rule. The Temple was, in a sense, a government building, as it had been rebuilt by King Herod the Great. To some Jews, it was as if God had been "kidnapped" and confined within the Temple by the tyranny of those who kept His people captive.

But wait: God doesn't dwell in a temple erected by human beings! King Solomon recognized that the day he inaugurated the Temple he had built. In his prayer of dedication, Solomon acknowledged the greatness of God and said: *"But will God really dwell on earth with humans? The heavens, even the highest heavens, cannot contain you. How much less this temple I have built!"* (2 Chronicles 6:18)

Hundreds of years later, the martyr Stephen declared: *"The Most High does not live in houses made by human hands."* He then quoted the prophet Isaiah: *"Heaven is my throne, and the earth is my footstool. What kind of house will you build for me? says the Lord. Or where will my resting place be?"* (Acts 7:48, 49)

The glory of God

At the time of Jesus' earthly ministry, Israel had lived under the authority of a king since the days of Saul. Now Herod Antipas, a son of Herod the Great, was the ruler of Galilee; the Caesar, Tiberias, ruled the whole Roman Empire.

A number of different objects—a crown, a scepter, a throne— symbolize the high dignity of a monarch. The throne represents the preeminence of the one who occupies it. The crown symbolizes the honor due the monarch, and the scepter represents authority.

Louis XIV, one of the most powerful rulers in Europe in the 17th century, ordered that a portrait be painted to commemorate his coronation. The artist, Hyacinthe Rigaud, used symbolic elements to depict the majesty of this proud French king and the opulence that surrounded him. Louis stands before an elegant curtain of crimson and gold; he carries a sword in a jewel–studded sheath; he is dressed in silken garments and a blue velvet robe lined with ermine and decorated with fleurs–de–lis, the emblem of the royal house of France. The crown appears on a cushion to the right of the king as he rests his hand on the scepter.

The Scriptures employ symbols to communicate the truth about God. For example, God reveals Himself in the likeness of a king.

> *In the year that King Uzziah died, I saw the Lord,*
> *high and exalted, seated on a throne; and the train of*
> *his robe filled the temple. Above him were seraphim,*
> *each with six wings: With two wings they covered their*
> *faces, with two they covered their feet, and with two they*
> *were flying. And they were calling to one another: 'Holy,*
> *holy, holy is the Lord Almighty; the whole earth is full of*
> *his glory.' At the sound of their voices the doorposts and*
> *threshholds shook and the temple was filled with smoke.*
> *'Woe to me!' I cried. 'I am ruined! For I am a man of*
> *unclean lips, and I live among a people of unclean lips,*
> *and my eyes have seen the King, the Lord Almighty.'*
> *(Isaiah 6:1–5)*

Here is an image of God as a sovereign, holding absolute authority, surrounded by glory and majesty. God, our Father, is far greater than any earthly king. He takes precedence over all creation. Angels adore and fear Him, and so must we.

The power of God

As I was writing these pages, the list of the richest people in the world was released. At the top of the list was Bill Gates, founder of Microsoft, with a fortune of over $78 billion, more money than many countries possess. However, this fortune—indeed, all the wealth of the world—is nothing compared to the possessions of our Lord God. The Bible declares, *"To the Lord your God belong the heavens, even the highest heavens, the earth and everything in it."* (Deuteronomy 10:14) This means that Mr. Gates, along with everything he has, belongs to God, who has allowed him to temporarily accumulate such riches.

I believe that when we pray, the Lord wants us to keep this in mind: God has absolute and irresistible power. He doesn't depend on anyone and doesn't ask permission of anyone. When He sets His mind to do something, nothing in the universe can stop Him. As "our Father who is in heaven," God is above all limitations and all earthly powers.

God can organize whatever is disorderly, restore what has been knocked down, illuminate what is in darkness, fill what is empty, and open what is closed. There is nothing He cannot do.

The uniqueness of God

"Hear, O Israel: The Lord our God, the Lord is one." (Deuteronomy 6:4) These words are at the very core of the Law of Moses and the faith of God's chosen people. To this day, they are repeated by practicing Jews every morning. Yet throughout the Old Testament, over and over, we see God's people—and, all too often, their kings—being seduced by despicable rituals as a means for solving their problems. They abandon their faith in the God

of heaven to go after idols of stone or wood made by human hands.

To most of us, such behavior is unthinkable. *"Is not God in the heights of heaven?"* (Job 22:12) Yet we all go through situations that tempt us to stray. Even people who have known the Lord for many years encounter circumstances in which their faith is tested. Our convictions are always at risk of being attacked. We are always in danger of being stripped of the treasures of our faith. As Jesus warned His disciples, *"The thief* [that is, Satan] *comes only to steal and kill and destroy."* (John 10:10)

When Jesus explained to His disciples the parable of the sower, He said, *"When anyone hears the message about the kingdom and does not understand it, the evil one comes and snatches away what was sown in their heart."* (Matthew 13:19) So it is not remarkable if on our journey to the New Jerusalem we sometimes ask ourselves questions such as these: Is the Bible truly God's Word? What about those passages that seem to contradict one another? Am I really in the truth? Could my family or my friends who practice a different religion be right? What if it turns out that after I die everything just ends there? In addition to accepting Christ as my Savior, do I have to become a member of a church and get involved in activities that take up so much time? Can't I live a "normal" life like everyone else and still go to heaven? Questions like these test our courage and our commitment as Jesus' disciples.

The world is full of pagan altars at which many worship: the altar of daily toil, where people focus their priorities on what to eat and drink and wear; the altar of worldly pleasures, where people engage in the worst excesses and debauchery; the altar of fame and fortune, where people seek satisfaction through pride and ambition and security in temporal riches; the altar of a permissive religion, where each one decides what to believe, what is good and what is bad. From all these altars, voices call to us like the Sirens of ancient Greek mythology, whose beautiful songs lured sailors into danger, causing their ships to crash on the reefs and sink. They seek to seduce us with sweet melodies which, once we are captivated, turn to discord and ultimate disappointment. *"There is a way that appears to be right, but in the end it leads to death."* (Proverbs 14:12)

The faithfulness of God

Have you ever felt surrounded by so many problems that they seemed like mountains? In Israel, many pilgrims who went to worship God in the Temple in Jerusalem were in danger of being assaulted and even killed while traveling on mountain roads to get to the city. This was a formidable test of their courage and commitment.

The writer of Psalm 121 seems to have been one of those pilgrims whose convictions were tested. He apparently felt anxious when he was traveling through those mountains, perhaps thinking of stories he had heard about travelers being attacked and imagining that the same thing could happen to him. Would anyone come to his aid? *"I lift up my eyes to the mountains,"* he wrote. *"Where does my help come from?"* (Psalm 121:1) His answer to that question has been a source of hope for countless believers throughout the centuries: *"My help comes from the Lord, the Maker of heaven and earth."* (Psalm 121:2)

Asaph was an Israelite totally devoted to God's service; his main task was to lead the praise in the Temple. He practically lived in God's house. Yet what he saw outside the Temple almost caused him to turn away from God: *"As for me, I almost lost my footing. My feet were slipping, and I was almost gone. For I envied the proud when I saw them prosper despite their wickedness."* (Psalm 73:2–3 *NLT*) Asaph began to wonder why some bad people seemed to have it so good. They neither feared nor respected God, yet they were healthy, lived comfortably, and accomplished all they set their minds to do.

In contrast, it seemed that many people who loved God—including Asaph himself—faced all kinds of difficulties, making it look as though they had been forgotten by Him. Asaph reached the point of asking, *"Did I keep my heart pure for nothing? Did I keep myself innocent for no reason? I get nothing but trouble all day long; every morning brings me pain."* (Psalm 73:13–14 *NLT*)

However, in the midst of his internal and external struggles, Asaph entered the Temple to pray and seek the God of heaven for answers to his questions. There he came to understand what the end reward will be both for those who are far from God and for those who live close to Him. This crisis of faith led Asaph to write one of the most beautiful declarations among the many found in the Psalms: *"Whom have I in heaven but you? I desire you more than anything on earth. My health may fail and my spirit may grow weak, but God remains the strength of my heart; he is mine forever."* (Psalm 73:25–26 *NLT*)

The benevolence of God

Television news and social media testify to the amazing, almost incredible lengths to which people will go when faced with a pressing need. Many put aside their moral and professional ethics, family values, patriotism, and religious vows to go after what they believe can give them security and solutions to their problems.

All of us, without exception, because of illness, disappointment, threats, loss, or misunderstanding and unfairness, have at some point felt helpless and hopeless. We feel that we are without resources, that we don't know what to do or whom to turn to. In times like these, we must remember that we are not alone, that we have a Father who will never abandon us and who knows our needs better than we do.

David described God's limitless knowledge in a very personal way: *"You know when I sit down and when I get up. You know my thoughts before I think them. You know where I go and where I lie down. You know everything I do."* (Psalm 139:2–3 NCV) Our Father knows and He cares and He acts.

God keeps bringing order into the lives of those who seek His help, restoring marriages and families in ruins, enlightening those who are bound in darkness and ignorance, filling empty hearts with love and hope, healing broken souls and suffering bodies, delivering people from addiction and transforming their lives. He is equal to every challenge, able to meet every need. Where human beings cannot, God can. He has acted on behalf of His children through all generations, and He hasn't changed.

What about you?

Where is your God? In a "temple," some special place where you go from time to time to listen to Him? At an altar in a corner of your home? Or do you worship the Father, who is in heaven? The challenge before you is never to lose sight of the greatness and goodness of God, in spite of your earthly struggles.

Jesus came to change mistaken human perceptions of God to that of an incomparable God, perfectly holy but also perfectly loving, available to all, profoundly understanding, and utterly able. In teaching His disciples to pray, Jesus communicated an essential truth, a foundation on which we can rest. *"Our Father who is in heaven"* knows and He cares and He acts.

Let us pray ...

Heavenly Father, I approach the majesty of your presence with humility. I have learned that although I am only human and have many limitations, I am not alone. I have learned that you are above all creation. Nothing can equal you in power, majesty, and glory—or in love. Just as angels do, I bow before you and declare that you are holy! holy! holy!

Thank you, Father, for sending your Son Jesus Christ to the world, because through Him I can get to know you better. I have a new hope, and my prayers can reach your throne. Now I can truly say: "Whom have I in heaven but you? I desire you more than anything on earth. My health may fail and my spirit may grow weak, but God remains the strength of my heart; he is mine forever."

Amen

4

"Hallowed be your name"

Honor your heavenly Father

THERE IS A WHOLE DISCIPLINE of linguistics devoted to studying the origin and meaning of names. It is called "onomastic" or "onomatology." (For example, my name, Alan, according to onomastic, means "good-looking, handsome.")

In many cultures in the Middle East, Africa, and Asia, personal names tend to have a meaning that reveals information about the individual's family or ethnic roots. Among Westerners, the meaning of names is not quite as relevant. We tend to choose a particular name because it is popular or unique, or because we like the way it sounds. Still, many people in Europe and North and South America are named in honor of a family member or a celebrity or as an act of devotion to a religious figure.

In the Bible, every name has a meaning. In many cases, a person's name is associated with his or her character and role. God used names to reveal His purposes and intentions for an individual, a nation, and even the whole of humanity. God changed Abram's name, which means "exalted father," to Abraham—"father of a multitude." He changed Jacob's name, meaning "deceiver," to

Israel, meaning "a prince with God." And He commanded that His Son be named Jesus, which means "the Lord saves."

These days, the names of important people can call to mind an immediate association, even if the name itself may not carry any significant meaning. For example, when someone mentions Mark Zuckerberg, we immediately think of Facebook. Elvis Presley is synonymous with rock and roll; Muhammad Ali with boxing; Babe Ruth with baseball. Pelé makes us think of soccer; Mother Teresa of charity; Adolf Hitler of genocide, and so on.

The Bible says that the name of God is *"glorious and awesome"* (Deuteronomy 28:58). When it is spoken, it evokes a range of thoughts and emotions: awe and wonder, love, fear, confusion, perhaps even anger. After all, human beings cannot fully know God. He is *"the blessed and only Ruler, the King of kings and Lord of lords ... who alone is immortal and lives in unapproachable light, whom no one has seen or can see. To him be honor and might forever."* (1 Timothy 6:15–16)

God's name commands honor

"To him be honor and might forever," Paul wrote. That's part of what Jesus was saying when He taught His disciples to pray, "hallowed be your name." In fact, some modern versions of the New Testament offer different translations of this line in Matthew 6:9: *"May your name be honored." (NET) "Help us to honor your name." (CEV)*

We must give to God's name the homage and honor it deserves. If we are to expect mercy and blessing from our heavenly Father, we must first recognize His greatness and His goodness.

Our God is great. The person of God is exalted and deserves

humble reverence. *"For this is what the high and exalted One says—he who lives forever, whose name is holy: 'I live in a high and holy place, but also with the one who is contrite and lowly in spirit, to revive the spirit of the lowly and to revive the heart of the contrite.'* "(Isaiah 57:15)

Our God is good. Every purpose of God is good from the moment He conceives it; therefore, we must be careful not to associate His name with evil. People often blame God for tragic situations or events that are the result of human irresponsibility or malice. There are also those who invoke the name of God to try to harm others or to practice occult rituals, which God forbids emphatically.

It is likely that many prayers vanish like steam in the air due to God's name being used wrongly. He is jealous of His person, and for a human creature to have the audacity and disrespect to use His name carelessly is a serious offense.

When we say the word "God," we should think about how small we are and how big He is.

> *But the Lord is the true God; he is the living God, the eternal King. When he is angry, the earth trembles; the nations cannot endure his wrath. ... God made the earth by his power; he founded the world by his wisdom and stretched out the heavens by his understanding. When he thunders, the waters in the heavens roar; he makes clouds rise from the ends of the earth. He sends lightning with the rain and brings out the wind from his storehouses. ... the Lord Almighty is his name. (Jeremiah 10:10, 12–13, 16)*

God's name represents authority

I grew up in a family in which the sense of authority was unmistakable. In Venezuela, where I was born, it is customary that when parents leave the house or come home, their children ask them for a blessing. But in our family, the younger siblings would also ask the older siblings for the blessing. This sign of respect is still maintained among my siblings, even though they have grown older. That respect derived from the hierarchical structure within the family. As a child, I was taught that my uncles, aunts, and grandparents had authority over me, and I had to obey them.

A missionary told of an occasion when some Christian schools in Bolivia were to be shut down by the government. A delegation led by the missionary went to the office of the minister of education to meet with him, but when they arrived, the secretarial assistant would not let them see the minister because they had no appointment. After conferring among themselves, the members of the delegation went back to the secretary and insisted that it was extremely important for them to see the minister.

During their conversation, the minister stepped out of his office for a moment and, seeing the missionary, said: "I know you. Where have we seen each other before?" The missionary reminded him that during an emergency some time before, the mission plane had been made available to transport the minister to a remote area of the country.

Then the minister asked, "What brings you here? May I help you with something?" The missionary informed him of the situation. Immediately, the minister took out his business card and said: "Don't worry. Go to the head office of the department and show them this card with my name. They will settle the matter." The name of the minister represented his authority over the education system throughout the country. When the missionary presented the minister's card, everything was resolved.

God's name tells us what we can expect from Him and how we should relate to Him. He rules the universe. His name represents dominion over all creation. Nature obeys Him; He can create, destroy, or restore. Angels obey Him; demons and the devil himself are subject to His commands. (See Job 1:12 and 2:6; Mark 1:34 and 5:12.) This means that, by virtue of being God, He is able to accomplish everything He sets out to do on our behalf. His name, rather than filling us with terror, should motivate us to please Him and worship Him *"with reverence and awe"* (Hebrews 12:28).

God's name reveals His eternal existence

Moses was alone with his thoughts on a mountainside, tending the flock of his father–in–law. Suddenly his attention was caught by a bush that was burning, but not burning *up.* Then he heard the voice of God issuing from the bush, calling his name. God commanded Moses to go to Egypt and lead His people, the Israelites, out of bondage. Moses resisted the idea, then said, "By the way, what's your name? If I do what you ask, the Israelites are sure to ask me, 'What is the name of this God you say has sent you to us?' "

"God said to Moses, 'I AM WHO I AM. This is what you are to say to the Israelites: "I AM has sent me to you."'" (Exodus 3:14) "I AM WHO I AM" is an attempt at an English translation of three words in the original Hebrew, which could also be rendered, "I WILL BE WHO I WILL BE." The name of God is a statement about His person. It

says that God is eternal, without beginning or end. That was the message to Moses and to the Israelites; it was the message to Jesus' disciples; it is the message for our time and for all time.

God revealed Himself to the Apostle John in these terms: *"I am the Alpha and the Omega … who is, and who was, and who is to come."* (Revelation 1:8) Alpha and Omega are the first and last letters of the Greek alphabet—the equivalent of "from A to Z." Many years after Moses' mountainside encounter with God at the burning bush, he would write these words: *"Before the mountains were born or you brought forth the whole world, even from everlasting to everlasting you are God."* (Psalm 90:2)

God had no beginning. He did not and does not need anyone or anything else to exist. The Athanasius Creed, an early statement of Christian doctrine, declares, "The Father is made of none; neither created, nor begotten." God has perfect, continuous, and endless life in Himself.

God's name signifies His holiness

To *hallow* God's name is to honor it. "Hallowed be your name" = "May your name be honored." *(NET)* But a more literal meaning of *hallow* is "to keep holy." "Hallowed be your name" = "May your name be kept holy." *(NLT)* Still another definition is "to set apart as holy." In fact, the words for "holy" in the Old Testament and the New literally mean "separate" or "set apart." In the Tabernacle in the wilderness, and later in the Temple in Jerusalem, there were places where the people could gather to worship. But there was an inner chamber called the Holy Place, where only priests were allowed to go; and within that chamber was another chamber called the Most Holy Place, where only the high priest could go, and only once a year. The Most Holy Place was set apart, utterly separate from the people.

At one time, the name of God was a mystery. When the word "mystery" is used in the Scriptures, it is not referring to something that can be investigated and figured out by finding the right clues, but something that is set apart by God and beyond knowing through natural means; it can be known only by divine revelation. For example, the Apostle Paul writes in several of his letters about a mystery *"which was not made known to people in other generations as it has now been revealed by the Spirit to God's holy apostles and prophets. This mystery is that through the gospel the Gentiles are heirs together with Israel, members together of one body, and sharers together in the promise in Christ Jesus."* (Ephesians 3:4–6)

God also revealed to Moses a mystery that had been hidden from earlier generations: His name. During the burning–bush encounter, God said His name was "I AM WHO I AM." Sometime later, He spoke again to Moses: *"I am the LORD. I appeared to Abraham, to Isaac and to Jacob as God Almighty, but by my name the LORD, I did not make myself fully known to them."* (Exodus 6:2–3) This doesn't mean that God has two names. The Hebrew word that is translated "LORD" is *Yahweh*, which is closely related to the word for "I AM." *(Jehovah* is another form of the word *Yahweh.)* God's name had been set apart as holy; now He revealed it as a sign that He was drawing near to His people.

God's name is holy. To hallow it, we must have a proper attitude of reverence and awe. We must recognize the vast gulf that separates God's name from any other name in heaven or on earth.

God commanded the Israelites: *"You shall not take the name of the Lord your God in vain, for the Lord will not hold guiltless anyone who takes his name in vain."* (Exodus 20:7 *NET)* Taking

God's name in vain doesn't refer only to swearing; it also means to use His name "thoughtlessly" (NCV) or "as if it were of no significance" (CEB). Using God's name in vain shows a profound lack of respect for Him.

Because of this commandment, the Jews were virtually terrified at the thought of pronouncing the name of God. Even today, Orthodox Jews are careful not to write or pronounce the full name directly, due to a fear of the possibility that they might "take His name in vain." God's name must be kept holy.

God's name proclaims His righteousness

God is absolutely holy; that means He is perfectly righteous. This is the fundamental difference between God and human beings—in fact, the very thing that separates them. *"The Lord looks down from heaven at the human race, to see if there is anyone who is wise and seeks God. Everyone rejects God; they are all morally corrupt. None of them does what is right, not even one!"* (Psalm 14:2–3 NET)

Here is a sampling of what God's righteousness looks like, in the language of the *Contemporary English Version:*

- He is a good God who always does the right thing. *"The Lord is a mighty rock, and he never does wrong."* (Deuteronomy 32:4)

- He is a truthful God who does not lie. *"God is no mere human! He doesn't tell lies or change his mind."* (Numbers 23:19a)

- He is a faithful God who is true to His word. *"God always keeps his promises."* (Numbers 23:19b)

- He is an unbiased God who ultimately gives each one what they deserve. *"Our Lord, you always do right, and your decisions are fair."* (Psalm 119:137)

- Except that: He is a compassionate God who loves to forgive those who seek Him. *"You don't stay angry forever; you're glad to have pity and pleased to be merciful."* (Micah 7:18–19)

- He is a gracious God who is kind to those who follow Him. *"You are wonderful, and while everyone watches, you store up blessings for all who honor and trust you."* (Psalm 31:19)

God is incorruptible and unchanging. He works according to His will. The Westminster Confession, prepared in 1646 at the request of the English Parliament, declares that God is "most free, most absolute; working all things according to the counsel of his own immutable and most righteous will."

To hallow God's name is not simply to acknowledge its holy character; we hallow God's name when our reverence is accompanied by a holy life. There are deeply religious people who take their beliefs very seriously but whose worship is not acceptable to God because their lives are not lived in accordance with His will.

The prophet Isaiah lived during a time of considerable spiritual decay among the people of Judah—God's people. A significant theme of the book that bears Isaiah's name is a repeated call to turn back to God. The vision the prophet had in the Temple in Jerusalem made it clear that he was to be a preacher of repentance. Isaiah saw the exalted Lord sitting on a throne and flanked by winged heavenly beings called seraphs. The word *seraph* means "burning one," suggesting the brilliant appearance of these beings, yet they hid their faces from the greater brightness of God's presence. The seraphs called out to one another, *"Holy, holy, holy, is the Lord Almighty; the whole earth is full of his glory."* (Isaiah 6:3)

Isaiah was terrified. He suddenly recognized the vastness of his separation from the divine perfection of God. He was overwhelmed by a realization of his unworthiness to behold that glory, and he cried out: *"I am ruined! For I am a man of unclean lips, and I live among a people of unclean lips."* (Isaiah 6:5) But then God, the very God who had just revealed His glory, revealed His mercy. One of the seraphs touched Isaiah's lips with a burning coal from the altar and said, *"See, this has touched your lips; your guilt is taken away and your sin atoned for."* (Isaiah 6:7) Then, immediately, God called Isaiah into ministry; and immediately Isaiah responded, *"Here am I. Send me!"* (Isaiah 6:8)

Unclean lips profane God's name

In our time, in everyday life, what are "unclean lips"? Imagine being with some friends when, suddenly, one of them starts to tell jokes with sexual content, using vulgar language. It's all too easy to get involved in a conversation like that and, without much thought, use the same kind of language. In a conflict with a spouse, a child, or any close relative, getting carried away by anger might result in the use of foul, nasty language. The Bible says, *"Do not let any unwholesome talk come out of your mouths."* (Ephesians 4:29)

Unclean lips are also those that are quick to express judgment, insults, or curses toward others. James throws the following exhortation at us, pointing out that it is contradictory in the extreme that the same lips that open to hallow God's name should also be unclean enough to open to attack others.

> *No human being can tame the tongue. It is a restless*
> *evil, full of deadly poison. With the tongue we praise our*
> *Lord and Father, and with it we curse human beings,*
> *who have been made in God's likeness. Out of the same*
> *mouth come praise and cursing. My brothers and sisters,*
> *this should not be. Can both fresh water and salt water*
> *flow from the same spring? My brothers and sisters, can a*
> *fig tree bear olives, or a grapevine bear figs? Neither can*
> *a salt spring produce fresh water. (James 3:8–12)*

Unclean lips are also those that open to worship the Father in heaven and, almost with the next breath, open to worship something or someone other than God.

Isaiah records God's complaint against the nation of Judah: *"These people come near me with their mouth and honor me with their lips, but their hearts are far from me. Their worship of me is based on merely human rules they have been taught."* (Isaiah 29:13) When our worship becomes routine, God is not satisfied and our prayers become ineffective.

What about you?

How about your lips? Are they unclean? How have you been speaking? The experience of Isaiah that day in the Temple is a reminder of the forgiving, redemptive nature of God. David said, *"A broken and contrite heart, you, God, will not despise."* (Psalm 51:17) God recognized Isaiah's humility and contrition, and his unclean lips were sanctified by the heavenly touch. You may need to seek cleansing for your lips. Only the touch of God will deliver you from guilt and make you fit to hallow His name.

Perhaps, like many believers, you would never deliberately use language that might offend God's ears, but at times you become careless and neglectful. Here are some more words from David that you might want to make a regular part of your prayer life: *"Set a guard over my mouth, Lord; keep watch over the door of my lips."* (Psalm 141:3)

Take a moment to reflect on how you use the name of God. Do you do so in a way that honors Him, recognizing His authority as the eternal Father who is perfect in holiness and righteousness? The name of God should bring you to your knees in reverence and awe. At the same time, His name should communicate strength and hope to you. He invites your worship—and your prayers.

Let us pray …

> Our Father in heaven, I thank you for the privilege of meeting you by calling on your name. Thank you that in your name I find hope and rest, even when facing difficult, discouraging circumstances. When I pronounce your name, God, I proclaim your eternal nature, your authority in heaven and earth, but also your mercy and love, and that you are faithful in keeping your promises. Knowing that no one compares with you, I honor you as perfect in righteousness.
>
> When you look at me, Father, don't look at my mistakes and weaknesses; don't look at the impurity of

my lips. Look at the blood of your Son Jesus, which has cleansed me from all sin. Remind me of your Word and your Spirit and keep me from using your name in vain. My desire is that I might live to please you and to lift up your name, which is forever holy. Thank you, God, for being who you are, and that you do not change.

Amen

5

"Your kingdom come"

Pray for something better

YOU'RE DRIVING TO WORK AND you turn on the car radio, tuned to a music station devoted to the latest hits. As you strain to hear and interpret the words of the song that comes on, you gradually identify its theme: Life is not worth living. You change to a different station and hear a newscaster presenting an update on the current crisis in the Middle East. *Well,* you think, *at least it's something worth listening to.* Suddenly the traffic comes to a stop. In a few moments, you learn that there has been a fatal accident up ahead.

How do you feel about the world you live in? Do you have an alarm system in your home or have you thought about installing one? When your children leave for school, do you fear for their safety? When you go out on the street, do you feel nervous? If you see a stranger wandering around the neighborhood, are you tempted to call the police? Are you concerned about the threat of a terrorist attack? Do you trust politicians? If you're not happy with the way things are, do you think they will eventually improve?

The feeling that the world is a scary place is nothing new. Writing at the beginning of the Second World War, Rebecca West, an English novelist and journalist, made the following observation: "Were I to ... take a peasant by the shoulders and whisper to him, 'In your lifetime, have you known peace?' wait for his answer, shake his shoulders and transform him into his father, and ask him the same question, and transform him in his turn to *his* father, I would never hear the word 'Yes', if I carried my questioning of the dead back for a thousand years."[1]

The decades that followed underscored West's point. After World War 2, the United Nations was established to seek peace and prevent war; sadly, its efforts have been largely unsuccessful—and even contradictory at times, since in searching for peace it has supported military action. The period since the founding of the UN has seen endless international violence, ranging from bilateral and regional conflicts to all—out war on a massive scale.

Yet people of every generation have longed for lasting peace. And from time to time, in some segments of society, some people have come to believe it just might be possible.

An impossible dream

On April 19, 1968, the musical *Hair* opened in New York City. It ran for 1,700 performances on Broadway, with thousands more taking place across the nation. Its impact was phenomenal. Several songs from the musical became worldwide hits. One, "Aquarius," became an anthem of the late 60s and much of the 70s. It spoke

---

1   Rebecca West, "Yugoslavia in the 1930s," *Black Lamb and Grey Falcon,* 1941, Vol. 1.

of the dawning of a new age, when "harmony and understanding, sympathy and trust" would prevail.

"Aquarius" was more than just a hit song from a Broadway musical. For centuries, astrologers had predicted the "Age of Aquarius," also called the Golden Age. With the beginning of Aquarius—which was said to have begun in the mid–20th century—the world would finally achieve fulfilment of its unsatisfied desire for tolerance, harmony, trust, and joy.

One version of the credo runs as follows:

> *This Golden Age is destined to synthesize all religious*
> *regimes and free the minds of ignorance and delusion.*
> *Each human being will begin his or her individual*
> *journey within, and strive to become the new race of*
> *super conscious humans awakening seekers of Truth and*
> *the eternal Spirit, healing peoples of many tongues and*
> *nations in the process."*[2]

Aquarius was predicted to be an era of comradeship among human beings in which knowledge and wisdom would guide people to solve conflicts justly and seek the common good. Hundreds of thousands of people around the world, mostly young people, eagerly welcomed the news. Sadly, their high hopes were quickly dashed and replaced by deep disillusionment. The modern age looks radically different from their expectations.

The world seems to be torn apart, and forecasts are not encouraging. Television news reports make it clear that the picture is the same everywhere: extreme violence, gross inequality, out-

---

2   This statement appears on the web page: www.ka-gold-jewelry.com.

rageous corruption, armed conflicts, people being trafficked for sex and slavery, suicide epidemics, immorality and amorality and social decay. In short, chaos reigns.

A fall from heaven

It all started a long time ago. A story comes from the ancient past of a heavenly being called Lucifer, meaning "light–bringer." He is described as a "guardian cherub." Cherubim appear in the Scriptures surrounding the throne of God and proclaiming His holiness and majesty. It is clear that even among these exalted creatures, Lucifer occupied a position of the highest honor. God gave the prophet Ezekiel a revelation of the splendor of this beautiful being:

> *This is what the Sovereign Lord says: 'You were the seal of perfection, full of wisdom and perfect in beauty. ... every precious stone adorned you ... Your settings and mountings were made of gold; on the day you were created they were prepared. You were anointed as a guardian cherub, for so I ordained you. You were on the holy mount of God; you walked among the fiery stones.'* (Ezekiel 28:12, 13–14)

However, in an instant of eternity, everything changed. God had created these heavenly creatures, the cherubim, with free will, the ability to choose whether to obey or disobey Him—that is, to choose between good and evil. God would one day offer His earthly creatures, human beings, that same choice. In his pride and arrogance, Lucifer chose evil; he rebelled against God.

'You were blameless in your ways from the day you were created till wickedness was found in you. … you were filled with violence, and you sinned. So I drove you in disgrace from the mount of God, and I expelled you, guardian cherub, from among the fiery stones. Your heart became proud on account of your beauty, and you corrupted your wisdom because of your splendor. So I threw you to the earth; I made a spectacle of you before kings.'
(Ezekiel 28:15, 16–17)

Lucifer was filled with vanity to the point that, in his delirium, he thought he was the equal of his Creator. The prophet Isaiah described the delusions that had taken over Lucifer's mind as well as the consequences of his wicked intentions:

How you are fallen from heaven, O Lucifer, son of the morning! How you are cut down to the ground, you who weakened the nations! For you have said in your heart: 'I will ascend into heaven, I will exalt my throne above the stars of God; I will also sit on the mount of the congregation on the farthest sides of the north; I will ascend above the heights of the clouds, I will be like the Most High.'
Yet you shall be brought down to Sheol, to the lowest depths of the Pit. (Isaiah 14:12–17 NKJV)

Lucifer had exalted himself as high as can be imagined. He fell equally low. Yet God did not deprive him of all of his power.

Chaos on earth

Many theologians see telltale signs of the work of Lucifer in the Creation story. *"In the beginning God created the heavens and the earth. Now the earth was formless and empty ... "* (Genesis 1:1–2) God is a God of order. So it's hard to imagine that when God made the earth, He created it "formless and empty." The theologians believe that one of the first acts of mighty Lucifer after he was hurled down to earth from his high position in heaven was to stir up a condition of chaos on earth.

But God quickly overrode Lucifer's evil intention and established order on the earth. Once He had made the necessary preparations,

> *"God created human beings in his own image. In the image of God he created them; male and female he created them. Then God blessed them and said, 'Be fruitful and multiply. Fill the earth and govern it. Reign over the fish in the sea, the birds in the sky, and all the animals that scurry along the ground.' "* (Genesis 1:27–28 NLT)

God placed the stewardship of the earth in the hands of Adam and Eve. He endowed them with great intelligence and gave them the authority and the resources they needed to be in charge of all earthly creatures. As if that was not enough, God regularly talked with Eve and Adam face to face in that beautiful garden called Eden. What more could they ask for?

We don't know how long Adam and Eve lived in obedience to God and in fellowship with Him. But eventually there was trouble in paradise. Lucifer, the light–bringer, had become Satan, meaning "adversary." Not satisfied with living in disobedience to God himself, Satan set out to corrupt others. He appeared in Eden to plant seeds of rebellion. Sadly, he found fertile soil in Adam and Eve.

God had created these first human beings in His own image, desiring above all else to enjoy fellowship with them. But He had also given them free will, the ability to choose between good and evil—just as He had with the heavenly cherubim. Adam and Eve were deceived into following Satan and disobeying God. And the earth, which had been so abundantly blessed, became a cursed, increasingly hostile environment. Life became a daily struggle to survive; family relationships were tragically torn; and a process of moral degradation began, culminating in God's decision to wreak utter destruction. *"I will wipe from the face of the earth the human race I have created."* (Genesis 6:7)

God preserved Noah and his family from the devastation, and they became the progenitors of a new humanity ... but with the old nature. The Bible says that this nature carries the hallmark of Satan, who after the Fall took over the world and has dominated it ever since.

Jesus called Satan *"the prince of this world"* (John 12:31) and said that he comes *"to steal and kill and destroy"* (John 10:10). The fact that the world continues in a state of chaos is a clear indication that it is under Satan's power. Satan hates all of God's creation and works to cause as much damage as he can.

The kingdom of God

Despite Satan's strength and the vast extent of his domain, God has set a date when the kingdom of darkness will fall. The power Satan has enjoyed will end when Jesus comes again to establish His kingdom forever and ever. (Revelation 11:15)

From the beginning of His ministry, Jesus spoke about the "kingdom of God" or the "kingdom of heaven." His first message was, *"Repent! For the kingdom of heaven is at hand."* (Matthew 4:17 *NKJV*) The kingdom of heaven is the theme of many of Jesus' parables.

The Jews of Jesus' day were hopeful that with the arrival of the Messiah, the kingdom of Israel would be restored to the power and glory it had enjoyed during the reign of David and Solomon. After the feeding of the 5,000, the crowd even tried to proclaim Jesus as their king, but He would not allow it. (John 6:14–15) He told Pilate, *"My kingdom is not of this world."* (John 18:36) The Jews were in pursuit of an earthly, imperfect, vulnerable kingdom, but they were ignoring the wise counsel of the psalmist: *"Do not put your trust in princs, in human beings, who cannot save. … The Lord reigns forever."* (Psalm 146:3, 10) While Satan maintains his influence and humans continue in government, world chaos will not end. The solution will come with the arrival of a new kingdom—God's kingdom.

What is the kingdom of God? Ultimately, it is divine authority prevailing over every point and every creature of the universe; and it is all the good that is generated by God's rule. All of us who love God should be yearning for His rule. The petition in the prayer model given by Jesus—"your kingdom come"—must become a clamor for God's justice to be fully established and ruling unquestioned on earth as in heaven. Jesus' coming began the final phase of God's plan to restore universal justice and reestablish His reign of good over all creation.

The Apostle Paul wrote, *"I consider that our present sufferings are not worth comparing with the glory that will be revealed in us,"* and that *"the creation waits in eager expectation for the children of God to be revealed. … the creation itself will be liberated from its bondage to decay and brought into the freedom and glory of the children of God."* (Romans 8:18–19, 21) Believers are called to be active agents in the realization of this work of the liberation of all creation. That work—the final phase of God's plan of redemption—will be consummated upon the return of the Lord Jesus.

For believers, the kingdom of God must be more than the topic of an occasional Sunday sermon. The establishment of the government of the heavenly Father should be the everyday desire of each of His children. And the kingdom of God is not only a glorious future reality, but also a present–day possibility. If the kingdom of God is the predominance of His authority and the enjoyment of His blessings, we should pray for our heavenly Father to be the One governing our lives and for His righteousness to prevail in our communities, throughout our nation, and around the world.

Satan uses his demons to enslave people and to create chaos. We must cry out to God to send His angels to release captives and to restore peace, social justice, equity—all the values derived from the goodness of God. To desire the kingdom of God is to crave these things. It is to ask the heavenly Father: "Improve this world and my life within it." It is also a statement of our intent to live each day submitted to His will.

What about you?

If you are not satisfied with the world you live in, don't blame God. If everything around you seems to be getting worse, pray for the Father's kingdom to come. Ask God to be, once and for all, the One who rules. Dedicate yourself to interceding before the Heavenly Father, praying for Satan's dominion to cease and for God to take control, and you can be the means of significant change in your community. If your home is a mess, pray for God to take over. Of course, that means that you must submit to His commandments, live His way.

Many are still hoping for the arrival of the Age of Aquarius—or something like it; they live in the expectation that the alignment of the stars and planets will have some influence on human consciousness and that, spontaneously, peace will come and love will prevail. The Bible teaches otherwise, claiming that true peace and love are made possible only by direct intervention from God. God gave the prophet Isaiah a glimpse of the environment that will prevail when His kingdom is finally established, centered in the New Jerusalem.

> 'I will create new heavens and a new earth. The former things will not be remembered, nor will they come to mind. But be glad and rejoice forever in what I will create, for I will create Jerusalem to be a delight and its people a joy. I will rejoice over Jerusalem and take delight in my people; the sound of weeping and of crying will be heard in it no more. ... They will not labor in vain, nor will they bear children doomed to misfortune; for they will be a people blessed by the Lord, they and their descendants with them. Before they call I will answer; while they are still speaking I will hear. The wolf and the lamb will feed together, and the lion will eat straw like the ox, and dust will be the serpent's food. They will neither harm nor destroy on all My holy mountain,' says the Lord. (Isaiah 65:17–19, 23–25)

Evangeline Booth was a daughter of William and Catherine Booth, founders of The Salvation Army, and herself the leader of the movement for many years. She wrote these words:

The world for God! The world for God!
There's nothing else will meet the hunger of my soul.
I see forsaken children, I see the tears that fall
From women's eyes, once merry, now never laugh at all;
I see the sins and sorrows of those who sit in darkness;
I see in lands far distant, the hungry and oppressed.
But behold! On a hill, Calvary! Calvary!

The world for God! The world for God!
I give my heart! I'll do my part!
The world for God! The world for God!
I give my heart! I will do my part![3]

Jesus did His part by giving His life to save us; our heavenly Father will do His. What about you? Are you doing your part? Are you longing for the coming of God's kingdom? Are you praying for its coming? Or are things "just fine" as they are?

Let us pray ...

Heavenly Father, the world I live in is getting worse, and until you intervene, I see no solution. I pray, blessed Father, for you to take control. Stop once and for all the activities of Satan, who steals, kills, and destroys the earth. Defeat the plans of the devil! Let your authority prevail over all creatures of the uni-

---

3   *The Song Book of The Salvation Army, #933.*

verse; be the King of my life, take control of my family; send your angels to fight for my neighborhood; let my city be impacted by your power, so that peace and justice prevail. Let your kingdom come, O God. In Jesus' name I pray.

Amen

6

"Your will be done"

Give up what you want

DURING THE SUMMER WHEN I was a kid, I sometimes went to a cousin's ranch, where there were many cows and horses. One evening, I got to watch my cousin begin the process of breaking one of the horses.

The animal was nearly 3 years old and had spent its life so far just grazing in the fields. The horse was unaccustomed to the presence of humans and had virtually no relationship with its owner. Far from being able to obey orders, it had never even had a bit in its mouth.

After harnessing the horse, my cousin led it, with some difficulty, to the corral. I quickly realized that taming a horse is a challenging task. Horses become nervous very easily, and when they feel threatened, they may react aggressively. An attempt to place a harness on a horse is likely to provoke bucking and neighing.

The horse gradually submits to wearing the harness. Next, following a tamed animal, it must learn to walk, trot, and gallop, then get used to wearing a saddle. Eventually, the animal learns to recognize the voice of its master and obey orders. Weight will be added to the saddle little by little so that when a rider mounts it, the horse will find it easier to adapt to its new life as a domesticated animal. The process is complete when the horse is able and willing to behave according to the will of its master. Experienced trainers say that only a happy horse that is comfortable with its master will respond properly to commands.

We humans have a relationship with our Creator that is somewhat like that between a horse and its master. We are accustomed to living our lives isolated from Him, doing our own will. As we walk through life, we resist the idea of being harnessed and submissive. If we do become obedient to God, it is only reluctantly.

We like to be independent, and when something or someone threatens that independence, we become defensive or aggressive. If we allow God to come near to us, we try to make it clear that everything will be fine as long as we are allowed to do as we please. We can accept a God who walks alongside us, but not one who wants to take the reins and ride us, directing us on the path He wants us to take. We are devotees of our own religion: self–will. Our theme song is Frank Sinatra's big hit, "I Did It My Way."

God has the power to impose His will on us, but it is not in His nature to do that. God's plan for us is that we subject ourselves to Him and do His will voluntarily:

> *I will instruct you and teach you in the way you should go; I will counsel you with my loving eye on you. Do not be like the horse or the mule, which have no understanding but must be controlled by bit and bridle or they will not come to you. (Psalm 32:8–9)*

A living sacrifice: denying self

Jesus taught His disciples to pray to the Father, "Your will be done." A key to learning about the will of God is contained in the Apostle Paul's letter to the Romans.

> *I urge you, brothers and sisters, in view of God's mercy,*
> *to offer your bodies as a living sacrifice, holy and pleasing*
> *to God—this is your true and proper worship. Do not*
> *conform to the pattern of this world, but be transformed*
> *by the renewing of your mind. Then you will be able to*
> *test and approve what God's will is—his good, pleasing*
> *and perfect will. (Romans 12:1–2)*

Believers often say, "I want to know the will of God," and they may spend a lot of time in prayer asking God to reveal it. But God's will is not a mystery. He has revealed it openly, in clear, simple terms. God's will is His Word, and His Word is readily available to us in written form: the Bible. God's will is also revealed in what He gives us and what He denies us. And God speaks by the Holy Spirit and through brothers and sisters in Christ to reveal His will in specific situations. Billy Graham wrote, "The important thing is not to know what to do, but what we do with what we already know."

Obeying God's will is harder than determining God's will. It's so difficult for us to accept the idea of someone else's will being imposed on us! When I was 9 years old, I went to live with my Aunt Mystic. She was a good woman, but she was also very strict. She did not like to say things twice; if she had to repeat an order, some kind of punishment was sure to follow. They were simple commands such as "make your bed," "clean up the yard and water the plants," "don't go any farther than the corner," "come straight home after school," and so on. Still … I always disobeyed.

The Lord Jesus often challenged His disciples as to the degree of their commitment. He confronted them straight out: *"Whoever wants to be my disciple must deny themselves and take up their cross and follow me."* (Mark 8:34) After a particularly difficult teaching, when many of His followers deserted Him, Jesus asked the Twelve, *"Do you also wish to go away?"* (John 6:67 *NRSV*)

Jesus makes the same demand of us and asks the same question. One day, everyone will have to appear before God, and the judgment we are subject to will be based on what we have done— the decisions we have made with respect to the will of God.

A renewed mind: thinking right

In addition to urging his brothers and sisters to *"offer [their] bodies as a living sacrifice,"* the Apostle Paul said, *"be transformed by the renewing of your mind."* (Romans 12:1, 2) When our minds are renewed, we adopt new ideas and new ways of seeing our relationships with God and with our neighbors. Ways of thinking and acting that don't conform to the will of God are replaced with those He has set out in His word.

Only God, by His Spirit, can renew the mind. But for that to happen, we must repent; *repent* literally means "to change one's mind." If God is to *renew* our minds, we must first *change* our minds; we must decide to obey His will, to go His way rather than our own. Have you read the story of the man who wanted his two sons to go to work in his vineyard?

> *He went to the first and said, 'Son, go and work in the vineyard today.' He answered, 'I will not'; but later he*

changed his mind and went. The father went to the second and said the same; and he answered, 'I will go, sir'; but he did not go. (Matthew 21:28–30)

After telling this brief story, Jesus asked His listeners, *"'Which of the two did the will of his father?' They said, 'The first.'"* (Matthew 21:31) The first son's repentance led him to rectify his mistake and do the will of his father. Jesus went on to say that many who have committed grievous sins enter the kingdom of God because they changed their minds, changed their ways, and began to do the will of the Father. Others, who have made public pledges to obey God but have not, will be rejected.

A costly commitment: testing and approving God's will

According to the Apostle Paul, only those who have offered their bodies to God as a living sacrifice and allowed Him to renew their minds are in a position to *"test and approve what God's will is"* (Romans 12:2). People often try to determine the will of God so they can decide whether they want to obey it. But it doesn't work that way. You can't test God's will without being ready to submit to it. The commitment comes first; then comes the revelation of God's will and the opportunity to test it out—by following it.

Jeremiah lived in one of the most difficult and decadent periods in the history of the nation of Judah. The people had turned away from God and everyone was corrupted, including the rulers. The religious leaders were greedy and impious and the military officers and judges were unjust. For the prophet Jeremiah, fulfilling the will of God meant having to tell everyone to their faces: "You are wrong, sinners! Repent, or God's judgment will come upon you!" Following the will of God always means paying a price, and Jeremiah suffered the consequences of his faithfulness. His friends turned away from him. He was slandered, beaten, and imprisoned.

Who would want to be known as the "prophet of doom"? Jeremiah got tired of the criticism and contempt; he didn't want people to continue rejecting him; he didn't want to be persecuted anymore. Jeremiah's diary —chapter 20 of the book by that name—reveals his state of depression. He actually came to the point of writing, *"Cursed be the day I was born! ... Why did I ever come out of the womb to see trouble and sorrow and to end my days in shame?"* (Jeremiah 20:14, 18)

Understandably, Jeremiah began to wonder why it wasn't possible for him to serve God without getting into so much trouble. Maybe it would be better just to leave things as they were. There must be other jobs that are better than that of a prophet! Jeremiah had tested God's will and decided that he could no longer approve it. So he tried to put in his resignation.

> *But if I say, 'I will not mention his word or speak anymore in his name,' his word is in my heart like a fire, a fire shut up in my bones. I am weary of holding it in; indeed, I cannot. (Jeremiah 20:9)*

Jeremiah wanted to evade God's will and purpose for his life, but he couldn't. God had chosen him to be His prophet before he was born. (Jeremiah 1:4–5) When Jeremiah was still a very young man, God said to him, *"I have put my words in your mouth."* (Jeremiah 1:9) In the end, Jeremiah repented; he changed his mind, deciding that he valued the will of God more than life itself, and he resumed his ministry as a prophet. Everything around him was destroyed, just as he prophesied, but God preserved the life of His servant. In the end, God's will passes any test.

God's good will: trusting His love

The Apostle Paul said that God's will is *"good, pleasing and perfect"* (Romans 12:2).

First of all, God's will is *good*. Nothing our Father does or allows in His children's lives has a final objective of causing suffering.

Sometimes we may not like God's will, just as we might hate the taste of some life–saving medicine. We may think at times that what God asks of us sounds crazy—like walking around the walls of a city for seven days shouting, expecting that the walls will then collapse. We might even come to think that what God expects us to do goes too far, such as loving our enemies and blessing those who curse us.

Accepting and doing God's will means changing our way of thinking. The goodness of God's will is founded on our Father's unlimited love for His children. But His love has an eternal perspective: *"From everlasting to everlasting the Lord's love is with those who fear him."* (Psalm 103:17) He sees and knows and loves for eternity. We must accept everything He does or allows in our lives, not with an eye to the present, but with the expectation of a better future and an even better forever.

God's good will: the perfect example

Gethsemane was the decisive moment for the consummation of our salvation. At that moment, Jesus had complete understanding of the will of God and its consequences for the world—but also of its immediate consequences for Him in the ordeal that He would have to go through. Mark (14:34) tells us that Jesus was *"overwhelmed with sorrow,"* Luke (22:44) that He was *"in anguish"* and that an angel appeared to strengthen Him (Luke 22:43).

We don't know exactly what that angel said or did, but we know what encouraged Jesus to do God's will as an act of unconditional surrender: *"For the joy set before him he endured the cross, scorning its shame, and sat down at the right hand of the throne of God."* (Hebrews 12:2)

What did Jesus envision beyond the Cross that filled Him with joy? He saw Satan defeated; He saw His gospel preached through the centuries and around the world; He saw millions of souls saved from eternal damnation; He saw great miracles of healing and transformation and liberation; He saw the name of His Father glorified. As He knelt there in that garden, Jesus saw Creation itself restored to the order that God established in the beginning and He saw the saved living by His side for eternity. All this and more brought great joy to the heart of the Lord Jesus. So it was written that He would say, *"I delight to do your will, O my God."* (Psalm 40:8 *NRSV*)

Jesus is our example. We must never forget that God works in our favor and pursues our permanent well–being, all with the intention of giving us ultimate joy. Even when God's actions seem to make no sense to us, they serve the goal of helping us and blessing us. God's will is good.

If we live with that understanding, God's will for us as individuals and for all of creation becomes a beautiful design of the highest order that gratifies and satisfies us. Life is no longer just a sequence of random events through which we have to walk with patience and resignation, but rather a blessed project through which we anticipate that God will show us His glory.

God's pleasing will: making Him happy

The Apostle Paul said that God's will is *pleasing* as well as good and perfect. (Romans 12:2) God's will is good—for us, His children. It is pleasing—to *Him*. The Apostle Paul writes that God *"destined us for adoption as his children through Jesus Christ, according to the good pleasure of His will."* (Ephesians 1:5 *NRSV*) Another translation puts it this way: *"God had already decided to make us his own children through Jesus Christ. That was what he wanted and what pleased him."* (Ephesians 1:5 *NCV*) God's will is what pleases Him.

Jesus told His disciples to pray to the Father, "Your will be done on earth at is in heaven." Heaven is full of angels. Angels are very powerful beings, yet they submit unreservedly to God's will, with no objections, no arguments—"no ifs, ands, or buts"—and no delay. God calls the archangel Gabriel and tells him to bring a word of assurance to the prophet Daniel, or to carry an important message to Mary or Joseph, and he does. When Jesus is born, God orders a group of angels to form a choir and sing joyfully for some shepherds nearby, and they do. God sends an angel to Jesus to encourage Him before the torment of the Cross, and he goes. God orders an angel to see to the removal of the stone from the tomb where the body of the Lord is laid, and he does. (The word *angel* means "messenger.") God's will is done in heaven, period!

The angels of heaven exist for the sole purpose of pleasing God, and that's what we are here for as well. Of course, in the long run, God wants to please us too. (After all, God's will is good.) The point is that we please God by obeying His will.

God delights in obedience. From the very beginning of history, humankind has followed Adam down the path of disobedience. Jesus came and demonstrated another way to live, a way that would please His Father: *"I have come down from heaven not to do my own will but to do the will of him who sent me."* (John 6:38) That same way is available to us. We are mere mortals, yet we have the capacity, with the help of the Holy Spirit, to bring joy to the heart of God!

God's pleasing will: an object lesson

Through the prophet Jeremiah, the Lord gave His people an object lesson about pleasing Him by doing His will. God told Jeremiah to invite the Rechabite family to the house of the Lord, take them into one of the side rooms, and give them wine to drink. Jeremiah did as he was told. *"Then I set before the Rechabites pitchers full of wine, and cups; and I said to them, 'Have some wine.' But they said, 'We will drink no wine.'"* (Jeremiah 35:5–6 NRSV)

"What is going on with these people?" the world might ask. "Are they going to pass up the opportunity to drink for free? Don't they like to party?" The religious folk, on the other hand, would be thinking: "Don't these people know who they're dealing with? This is Jeremiah! Haven't they heard his preaching? Don't they realize that he's always predicting calamities? Doesn't it occur to them that he could prophesy against them for not obeying? He's giving them an order in the house of the Lord! Why don't they obey him?"

What was going on anyway? What did these people have to say for themselves?

> *Our ancestor Jonadab son of Rechab commanded us, 'You*
> *shall never drink wine, neither you nor your children;*
> *nor shall you ever build a house, or sow seed; nor shall*
> *you plant a vineyard, or even own one; but you shall live*
> *in tents all your days, that you may live many days in the*
> *land where you reside.' (Jeremiah 35:6–7 NRSV)*

The Rechabites went on to say that from that point on they had never drunk wine, never planted vineyards or raised other crops, and never built houses for themselves. They said, *"we have lived in tents, and have obeyed and done all that our ancestor Jonadab commanded us."* (Jeremiah 35:10 *NRSV)*

It appears that none of the Rechabites ever asked why. Why would living in tents, not growing their own food, and never drinking wine mean that they could live a long time in the land? They simply obeyed. God used their unquestioning, unhesitating obedience as an example. Speaking through Jeremiah, the Lord said to the people of Judah:

> *The command has been carried out that Jehonadab son*
> *of Rechab gave to his descendants to drink no wine; and*
> *they drink none to this day, for they have obeyed their*
> *ancestor's command. But I myself have spoken to you*
> *persistently, and you have not obeyed me. I have sent to*
> *you all my servants the prophets, sending them persis-*
> *tently, saying, 'Turn now every one of you from your evil*
> *way, and amend your doings, and do not go after other*
> *gods to serve them, and then you shall live in the land I*
> *gave to you and your ancestors.' But you did not incline*
> *your ear or obey me. The descendants of Jehonadab son of*

Rechab have carried out the command that their ancestor gave them, but this people have not obeyed me. (Jeremiah 35:14–16 NRSV)

The Rechabites remained faithful to the will of their ancestor, and did so for generations. Not even the command of the prophet Jeremiah caused them to compromise their vow of obedience. The obedience of the Rechabites pleased God, and He promised them that they would survive the destruction that was coming upon Jerusalem. His desire was—and is—that His people accord His will the same level of obedience.

God's perfect will: acknowledging His supremacy

Looking once again to the Apostle Paul, we see that the will of God, which is good and pleasing, is also *perfect*. (Romans 12:2) God's will is a manifestation of His desires and designs; therefore, it must be perfect. Whatever God thinks or does cannot be improved upon; when He makes a decision and takes action, there is no better option or possibility. King Solomon put it this way: *"I know that everything God does will endure forever; nothing can be added to it and nothing taken from it."* (Ecclesiastes 3:14)

God does not change with time (Malachi 3:6); He is immutable and constant, not only regarding His person, but also in His purposes (James 1:17). Further, God's will is righteous, with no evil in it. David the psalmist wrote:

> *The law of the Lord is perfect,*
> *refreshing the soul.*
> *The statutes of the Lord are trustworthy,*

> *making wise the simple.*
> *The precepts of the Lord are right,*
>   *giving joy to the heart.*
> *The commands of the Lord are radiant,*
>   *giving light to the eyes.*
> *The fear of the Lord is pure,*
>   *enduring forever.*
> *The decrees of the Lord are firm,*
>   *and all of them are righteous.*
>
> (Psalm 19:7–9)

Nothing is left to chance or coincidence in God's will. It's like a perfectly synchronized machine, processing the raw materials that are the circumstances we face in life. Those circumstances become experiences that shape our character and help us trust God and realize that He is in control at all times. Our heavenly Father, with all His power, is able to use any event—whether illness, accident, temptation, enemy attack, financial emergency, loss, persecution, family conflict—for our benefit. *"We know that in all things God works for the good of those who love Him, who have been called according to his purpose."* (Romans 8:28)

However, the will of God is not some kind of unknown force acting inevitably on our destiny. A fatalistic view of God's will, in which everything that happens is predetermined—for good or ill—and the only possible response is passive resignation, is utterly wrong. The working of God's will in our lives requires cooperation on our part, with full confidence in the truth of this word: *"Walk in obedience to all I command you, that it may go well with you."* (Jeremiah 7:23)

God's perfect will: rejoicing in His lordship

Mary was a young Jewish woman who was engaged to be married to a man named Joseph. In her time and place, engagement was much more than a statement of intent. In fact, in the eyes of their community, Mary and Joseph were regarded as married, except that it was understood that the relationship would not be consummated until after the wedding ceremony had taken place and the couple were living together. Mary was fully committed to her promise to devote herself exclusively to Joseph. But one day, when she least expected it, God exercised His sovereign will and Mary became pregnant.

When the angel Gabriel visited Mary and gave her the "good news," her first reaction was the obvious one: *"How can this be, since I am a virgin?"* (Luke 1:34 *NRSV*) The angel's answer was astounding: the Holy Spirit would cause her to conceive, and the child she bore would be the Son of God. Mary's unhesitating response rings through the ages as a prime example of submission to the will of God: *"Here am I, the servant of the Lord; let it be with me according to your word."* (Luke 1:38 *NRSV*)

Even at her young age, Mary was a woman of great faith and devotion to God. Still, questions must have swirled in her head: *What will the neighbors think when they see that I am pregnant? What can I say to them? Who would believe me? And my beloved Joseph! Will he want to break off our engagement?*

Mary may have *thought* of all these things, but she *knew* one central thing: God's will is *perfect*; and if it was *pleasing* to Him to use her in this way, it would be *good* for her. Indeed, it would be far beyond good. It would be a high honor, and that brought great joy to Mary's heart.

And Mary said: 'My soul magnifies the Lord, and my spirit rejoices in God my Savior, for he has looked with favor on the lowliness of his servant. Surely, from now on all generations will call me blessed; for the Mighty One has done great things for me, and holy is his name.' (Luke 1:46–49 NRSV)

What about you?

Would you be willing, like Mary, for God to make you an example of obedience to His will? You might not be chosen person of the year by *TIME* magazine. You might not appear on television or even on the front page of your local newspaper. But you could be an example to your family, your friends, your neighbors, your coworkers or classmates, and your fellow believers. Imagine God bragging about you as He once did about another one of His children: *"Have you considered my servant Job? There is no one on earth like him; he is blameless and upright, a man who fears God and shuns evil."* (Job 1:8)

Don't forget that God's will is good. Obeying Him brings its own reward. The Apostle John says, *"The world and its desires pass away, but whoever does the will of God lives forever."* (1 John 2:17)

Being in God's will ensures ultimate satisfaction; outside of it, hope is impossible. Do you want God to take control of the reins of your life? He says: *"Come to me, all you who are weary and burdened, and I will give you rest. Take my yoke upon you and learn from me, for I am gentle and humble in heart, and you will find rest for your souls. For my yoke is easy and my burden is light."* (Matthew 11:28–30) Will you say, "Your will be done"?

Let us pray …

Heavenly Father, I come to you well aware that, in myself, I am not worthy to be received or heard. You are the everlasting God, the Lord of the universe; I am a rebellious creature, always ready to do my own will. Yet you say that you love me. Today I have heard your voice, and I have decided to obey your will. With your help, I am ready to follow you, whatever the cost, whatever the circumstance, until the last day I am in this world. Sustain me in the midst of the trials life presents me. Thank you, thank you for your mercy. In the name of Jesus Christ I pray.

Amen

7

"Give us this day our daily bread"

Take one day at a time

I STILL RECALL VIVIDLY THE image of a man who lived in the neighborhood where I spent the early years of my life. People called him "the cannibal." He was a short man with thick black hair, white skin, and a round, smiling face. No one could imagine that he was capable of doing what was said about him.

The man had been in jail several times, convicted of robbery. Finally he was sent to El Dorado, a terrible prison in the Venezuelan Amazon where the most dangerous criminals are incarcerated. The prison is in a remote jungle area, surrounded by rivers infested with piranhas and alligators. People said that it would be virtually impossible to escape from there; but this man escaped with two other convicts.

When the man was captured, he told of the odyssey he and his companions lived through after their escape. Hunger made them go almost insane, and to survive, two of them killed the third and ate part of his body. Thereafter, until his death, this man was known as "the cannibal."

Viktor Frankl, a psychiatrist, was interned in a Nazi concentration camp during World War 2. He studied the responses of his fellow prisoners to the conditions of that environment, including their reaction to hunger. Frankl wrote: "Those who have not gone through a similar experience can hardly conceive of the soul–destroying mental conflict and clashes of will power which a famished man experiences."[1]

Hunger is one of the strongest compulsions a human being can experience. All other appetites and desires lose relevance in the face of the need for food. God knows it; He created us with this need. Jesus also knows it; He experienced the physical pangs and emotional anxiety generated by extreme hunger during His days in the wilderness before the beginning of His earthly ministry.

Food for the body

Human beings are unique in the universe. God created millions of species of animals with bodies of all different shapes and sizes, but not the ability to reason or have moral judgment or complex emotional feelings. He created the angels as spirits. However, He equipped human beings with minds of superior intelligence and souls that can appreciate the divine—and gave us bodies as well. The body sets us apart from the angels.

In an overreaction to the Apostle Paul's teaching that we are to *"set our minds on things above, not on earthly things"* (Colossians 3:2), some believers have a tendency to devalue the human body, to think of it as essentially "unholy" or, at best, of little importance. But this is not what the Scriptures teach. Jesus Himself valued the human body as one of God's finest creations. He demonstrated this

---

1   Viktor E. Frankl, *Man's Search for Meaning* (Beacon Press, 1959).

when He assumed human bodily form in the fetal stage and lived the whole process of biological development—infancy, childhood, adolescence, and adulthood—just like you and me.

The human body is created by God. It is *"fearfully and won-derfully made"* (Psalm 139:14). And, by God's design, it needs food to survive.

Some have wondered why God didn't create us with the ability to exist without food. Ultimately, like many such questions, this one can only be answered this way: God's wisdom and God's sovereignty are absolute. In this, as in all things, He knew what He was doing.

Charles H. Spurgeon said in one of his sermons:

> God is a sovereign. ... When He had resolved to
> make man, He had a right to make him whatever
> kind of creature He liked. ... When He made him,
> He had a right to put any command on him that He
> pleased. And God had a right to say to Adam, 'You
> shall not touch that forbidden tree.' And when Adam
> offended, God had a right to punish him and all the
> race forever in the bottomless pit! ... He has a right
> to do just as He pleases with us.[2]

Before they sinned, Adam and Eve had no need to ask God for "daily bread"; it was guaranteed to them. *"The Lord God made all kinds of trees grow out of the ground—trees that were pleasing to the eye and good for food."* (Genesis 2:9) Here were trees they didn't have to plant in a garden they didn't have to care for; delicious,

---

2   C. H. Spurgeon, Selected Sermons (Metropolitan Tabernacle Pulpit).

nutritious fruits in abundance, all at their fingertips. However, one tree bore forbidden fruit; and Eve and Adam, exercising their God–given free will, ate of that tree. Their disobedience changed everything. From that point on, food could be obtained only at the cost of "painful toil," wrenched from ground that God had cursed. (Genesis 3:17-19) The preservation of life itself became a constant struggle.

Food for tomorrow?

Jesus told a parable about a rich man whose fields yielded an unusually large harvest. He thought to himself, "I'm running out of space to store my crops. I'd better tear down my barns and build bigger ones so I have enough room for the surplus." *"'And I'll say to myself, "You have plenty of grain laid up for many years. Take life easy; eat, drink and be merry."' But God said to him, 'You fool! This very night your life will be demanded from you. Then who will get what you have prepared for yourself?'"* (Luke 12:19–20)

The history of the United States in the 20th century offers a prime example of the folly of assuming that the prosperity of today can be depended on for tomorrow. In the 1920s, the nation's economy was booming, and optimism about the future rose along with it. Herbert Hoover ran for president in1928 with the promise: "A chicken in every pot and a car in every garage." Everyone, including many economists, thought the future was secure.

Then came the stock market crash of October 1929. Within a month, $30 billion disappeared. Thousands of companies went bankrupt and a quarter of the working population, about 15 million people, were unemployed.

By 1932, 25 percent of the banks had gone broke, and more

than 9 million people saw their savings vanish. Members of the middle class sold their jewelry and their furniture to survive, then resorted to loans they couldn't repay. Eventually, many were forced to move to the slums.

Sales ads for homes and businesses appeared everywhere, but no one was buying. More than 750,000 farmers lost their crops and animals and, eventually, their land; as a result, thousands migrated to the cities, which intensified urban unemployment and poverty. Many people were willing to work in exchange for just food. Suicide and crime rates reached record levels.

Children were among the hardest hit. Many schools closed because the children had to earn money to help their families. Milk consumption decreased and diseases among children increased.

On streetcorners in large cities, it was common to see men, women, and children begging. The government had to convert large warehouses into shelters and soup kitchens where thousands of people lined up to get a bowl of soup and a piece of bread.

Not until the Second World War did these disastrous conditions come to an end.

No one but God can see the future. God alone has the power to grant or guarantee tomorrow.

> *Now listen, you who say, 'Today or tomorrow we will go to this or that city, spend a year there, carry on business and make money.' Why, you do not even know what will happen tomorrow. What is your life? You are a mist that appears for a little while and then vanishes. Instead, you ought to say, 'If it is the Lord's will, we will live and do this or that.' (James 4:13–15)*

The teaching of God's Word should be reason enough for us to leave the future in God's hands. Jesus said, *"Do not worry about tomorrow, for tomorrow will bring worries of its own."* (Matthew 6:34 *NRSV)*

Food for today

Jesus did not teach His disciples to ask for bread for tomorrow. He taught them—He teaches us—to ask the Father "this day" for our "daily bread." That means enough for today, and no more. The Lord spoke of material food, but I believe "bread," in this context, refers not only to food, but also to the means and resources we need in order to live. Praying with this idea in mind is an expression of total surrender to the Father's care.

The way in which God cares for His people every single day is amply illustrated in the way He sustained the Israelites in the desert. It has been estimated that more than a million people went out of Egypt headed for the land of Canaan. A month and a half into their journey, the people complained that they were about to die of hunger. God said to Moses:

> *'I will rain down bread from heaven for you. The people are to go out each day and <u>gather enough for that day</u>. In this way I will <u>test them</u> and see whether they will follow my instructions. On the sixth day they are to prepare what they bring in, and that is to be twice as much as they gather on the other days.' (Exodus 16:4–5)*

God wanted to see how much His people trusted Him. Sadly, some of them ignored His instructions that they should gather only enough for each day. Their disobedience showed that they doubted God's word. And the bread—called "manna"—that they had saved for later bred maggots and started to stink.

Will God provide for His children today? The answer is a resounding "Yes!" And the basis on which God provides "daily bread"—with all that that implies—is simply this: trust in Him.

The single parent can trust the heavenly Father for His provision; so can those who, because of physical limitations or because of limited opportunities, cannot work for a living; the low–income family, those who just never seem to have enough money; and men and women who devote their lives to full–time service for the Lord. For all who trust God, the testimony of the Psalmist David rings true: *"I was young and now I am old, yet I have never seen the righteous forsaken or their children begging bread."* (Psalm 37:25) God is the source of all provision. The Apostle Paul adds this promise: *"My God will meet all your needs according to the riches of his glory in Christ Jesus."* (Philippians 4:19)

Edward M. Bounds, the great exponent of prayer, wrote:

> When we pray, 'Give us this day our daily bread,'
> we are, in a measure, shutting tomorrow out of our
> prayer. We do not live in tomorrow but in today. We
> do not seek tomorrow's grace or tomorrow's bread.
> ... Bread, for today, is bread enough. Bread given for
> today is the strongest sort of pledge that there will be
> bread tomorrow.[3]

---

3   E.M. Bounds, *The Necessity of Prayer* (first published 1929; available from Amazon.com).

Food for the soul

"Our daily bread" is essential for subsistence. However, in response to temptation, Jesus quoted the book of Deuteronomy: *"One does not live by bread alone, but by every word that comes from the mouth of God."* (Matthew 4:4 *NRSV*) The Apostle Paul warned about people whose *"god is their stomach"* (Philippians 3:19).

One of Jesus' most outstanding miracles was the multiplication of the loaves and fishes to satisfy the hunger of the crowd of people who had come to listen to Him. The following day, the crowd chased after Jesus, not because they believed in Him as the Messiah but because they hoped to receive more food. But Jesus said to them, *"Do not work for food that spoils, but for food that endures to eternal life."* (John 6:27) He went on to explain:

> *'I am the bread of life. Whoever comes to me will never go hungry, and whoever believes in me will never be thirsty. ... I am the living bread that came down from heaven. Whoever eats this bread will live forever.'* (John 6:35, 51)

Earthly bread spoils, but not the bread of Heaven. Sustenance for eternal life depends on Jesus Christ.

The primary purpose of prayer, after all, is not to ask God to satisfy our wants or even to meet our needs. An examination of Jesus' teaching on prayer up to this point makes this abundantly clear.

- *"Our Father ... "* First, we are to recognize God as our Father—the source of all creation, visible and invisible, who nevertheless desires an intimate relationship with each of us.

- *"Who is in heaven ... "* We are to extol the greatness of God's power and the eminence of His position in heaven, from which He exercises His authority.

- *"Hallowed be your name."* We are to exalt the honor and holiness of God's name and all that it reveals of His nature and attributes.

- *"Your kingdom come."* We are to beseech God for the manifestation of His kingdom in our lives and in our world and seek the final establishment of His absolute sovereignty over all things.

- *"Your will be done."* We are to confess our faith that God's intentions are perfect and designed for our good and declare our humble submission to His will.

If we consistently pray in this way, we can confidently put aside all concern for our personal needs. Luke notes that Jesus exhorted the disciples with these words: *"Seek the kingdom of God, and all these things shall be added to you."* (Luke 12:31 *NKJV)* The "things" of which Jesus was speaking are food, clothing, shelter—all that is needed for the preservation of life.

"You are what you eat" has become a common expression. Spurgeon said:

> When a man can say, 'My hope is in the Crucified alone' … then he has got the meat indeed! He will be a strong man to overcome his sin! He will be a holy man, a happy man, a heavenly man and, by–and–by, he shall be caught up to dwell where Jesus is, on whom he has fed.[4]

---

4   C. H. Spurgeon, *Selected Sermons* (Metropolitan Tabernacle Pulpit).

What about you?

What are your prayers like? Are they anything like the model Jesus gave His disciples? It's absolutely right for you to ask God to give you your "daily bread." That doesn't necessarily mean, of course, that He will rain bread down from heaven, as He did for the Israelites in the desert. More likely, you or someone in your family—like Adam and all who have followed him—will have to get your bread *"by the sweat of your brow"* (Genesis 3:19). So your prayer might take the form of asking God to open up opportunities for work that allows you to earn enough to meet your needs. You might ask Him to deliver you from illness or accidents that would limit your ability to work. And so on.

But do you begin by acknowledging and praising God's virtues and sublime attributes? Or do the pressures of daily needs, or of a situation that suddenly arises, get in the way of that? Starting right—lifting up the person and the name of God in worship and praise and confessing your determination to obey Him in all things—serves as an acknowledgment of what you know to be true: Your heavenly Father is in control. He loves you. And He can and will meet your every need.

Let us pray...

> Dear heavenly Father, thank you that in spite of
> my mistakes, you invite me to come to you. Thank
> you that in your great mercy you have said that you
> will meet all my needs. Before you now, I make the
> decision to trust your promises. Give me the wisdom
> to put my eyes on things above, which are eternal,

and not on things of the earth, which are temporary. Compassionate Lord, I ask that my table may have bread today. I leave tomorrow in your hands. Thank you for Jesus Christ, the true bread from heaven, in whose name I pray these things.

Amen

8

"Forgive us our debts ... "

Recognize when you are wrong

WHEN I WAS BEGINNING TO work on this chapter, the science fiction movie *Planet of the Apes* was being shown on television. (I was 11 years old when it was first released in theaters.) The movie had a terrific impact and spawned several sequels as well as a very successful TV series. A slogan used to promote the film was, *"Somewhere in the universe there must be something better than man."*

That sounds rather insulting. We like to think we are pretty good—or at least not too bad. The philosophers of the 18th–century Enlightenment proclaimed that human beings were supreme in the universe and good by nature. Going through life thinking otherwise is uncomfortable, like having a pebble in your shoe.

But, laying history aside, think about the common atrocities of our own time: abuse and exploitation of women and children; drug dealing; abortion; mass shootings; murder within families; violation of human rights in its various manifestations—racism, sexism, terrorism in the name of religion, trafficking of bodily organs and of human beings, genocide and slavery in countries around the globe. Taking all that into consideration ... are we good by nature?

King Solomon mused about this question and concluded, *"This alone have I discovered: God made humankind upright, but they have sought many evil schemes."* (Ecclesiastes 7:29 *NET)*

We can rationalize and argue that circumstances cause us to do things we shouldn't do. "I had to lie to avoid getting fired from my job"; "I stole because I had nothing to eat"; "I'm in prostitution to pay my college tuition." But we know better. The human conscience is an ever-present reminder of our moral responsibility.

We are all sinners

"The Lord looks down from heaven at the human race, to see if there is anyone who is wise and seeks God. Everyone rejects God; they are all morally corrupt. None of them does what is right, not even one!" (Psalm 14:2–3 *NET)*

A believer might well respond to this judgment and say, "Well, I'm not quite *that* bad! It's not like I *never* do anything right." But that's not the point. The response from Scripture: *"There is not one truly righteous person on the earth who <u>continually does good and never sins</u>."* (Ecclesiastes 7:20 *NET)* We must never make the mistake of thinking we are blameless. *"If we claim to be without sin, we deceive ourselves and the truth is not in us."* (1 John 1:8) Or, as the Apostle Paul put it, *"All have sinned and fall short of the glory of God."* (Romans 3:23) If we think of sinning as falling short of God's glory, the matter begins to come clear.

Some of us may sin more often than others, but we all sin. Even though we may have been truly converted, we struggle daily with internal and external forces that are determined to move us away from the will of God. The Apostle Paul wrote about this struggle in very personal terms in Romans 7. He advised: *"If you think you are standing firm, be careful that you don't fall!"* (1 Corinthians 10:12) No one is exempt from moments of weakness. Jesus said, *"Watch and pray so that you will not fall into temptation. The spirit is willing, but the flesh is weak."* (Matthew 26:41)

Even the most dedicated and holy Christians, at some point in their lives, give in to their weaknesses. It's actually a relief to recognize that this was true of our Bible heroes as well. Charles Swindoll says, "All the men and women of Scripture have feet of clay, and when the Holy Spirit paints a portrait of their lives, He's a very realistic artist. He doesn't ignore, deny, or overlook the dark side."[1]

We are all sinners: A case study

In a certain city lived a young man of humble origins but of great integrity. He was married to a beautiful young woman; however, before they could have their first child, the young man was called on to join the army. The country was at war, and he was sent to the battlefront.

During this time, an extraordinary leader ruled the country. He was hailed as a great warrior and military commander. He was also a fine musician and poet. He had been blessed with a large family. He was successful in everything he undertook and had everything a person could want. Most important, this king feared God and tried to live in a way that would please Him.

Ordinarily, such a king would have led his army into battle. On one particular occasion, however, the monarch did not go.

One evening, he walked out on the roof of his palace, seeking

---

1   Charles Swindoll, *David* (Thomas Nelson, 1997; available from Amazon.com).

relief from the heat of the day. From the rooftop he saw a beautiful young woman bathing. The king asked a servant to find out who the woman was, and learned that she was the wife of the young soldier. Because he was the king and had the power to do so, he sent messengers to bring her to the palace. He made her go to bed with him; then she went home.

After some time, the young woman sent a message to the king: "I am pregnant." So the king commanded that her husband be brought back from the battlefield to the palace. The king provided a lavish dinner for the young man and asked him for a report on how the war was going. Then he told the soldier to go home for the night and sleep with his wife. The king was hoping that later on, when the young man learned that his wife was pregnant, he would believe that the child to be his. However, the young soldier felt it would be wrong to go home to sleep and delight himself with his wife while his comrades were enduring danger and discomfort in the battlefield. He slept at the entrance to the palace with the king's servants.

When the king saw that the situation was getting complicated, he made a shocking decision—shocking because it would not be expected of a man whom God had blessed so richly and had once called "a man after His own heart." The king wrote a letter to the general of his army, sealed it, and sent it to the battlefront with the soldier himself. The letter told the general to put the young man at the front of the battle line where the fighting was the hottest, then pull back from him so he would be killed. That is exactly what happened. The honest, loyal young soldier—whose name was Uriah—was killed.

Some time later, the king—whose name was David—ordered that the young woman—whose name was Bathsheba—be brought to the palace, and he took her as one of his wives. That seemed to be the end of the story. However, the king had forgotten one important detail: The Lord's eyes *"are on the ways of mortals; he sees their every step. There is no deep shadow, no utter darkness, where evildoers can hide."* (Job 34:21–22)

Sin has consequences

The Bible tells what happened next. There was a prophet in Israel, a man called Nathan. The Lord sent Nathan to David, and the prophet told the king a story about two men, one rich and one poor. The rich man had many flocks and herds; the poor man had just one little lamb that he treated as a pet and deeply loved. A traveler came to the rich man's house for a visit, and the rich man wanted to prepare a meal for him. But instead of taking one of his own sheep or cattle, he took the little lamb from the poor man, killed it, and prepared the meal for his visitor.

> *David burned with anger against the man and said to Nathan, 'As surely as the Lord lives, the man who did this must die! He must pay for that lamb four times over, because he did such a thing and had no pity.'*

> *Then Nathan said to David, 'You are the man! This is what the Lord, the God of Israel, says: "I anointed you king over Israel, and I delivered you from the hand of Saul. I gave your master's house to you ... And if all this had been too little, I would have given you even more. Why did you despise the word of the Lord by doing what is evil in his eyes? You struck down Uriah the Hittite*

with the sword and took his wife to be your own. You
killed him with the sword of the Ammonites. Now,
therefore, the sword will never depart from your house,
because you despised me and took the wife of Uriah the
Hittite to be your own.'

'This is what the Lord says: "Out of your own household
I am going to bring calamity on you. Before your very
eyes I will take your wives and give them to one who is
close to you, and he will sleep with your wives in broad
daylight. You did it in secret, but I will do this thing in
broad daylight before all Israel." ' (2 Samuel 12:5–8a,
8c–12)

When David's sin was exposed, he was in deep distress, overwhelmed by feelings of guilt and shame and remorse. His smile faded, replaced by a look of dejection. His harp, which for more than 20 years had filled the palace with beautiful melodies, stopped ringing; his voice, which had so often sung praise to the good and merciful God, fell silent. He sought peace and could find no peace. This is the consequence of sin.

I imagine that every time David thought to walk out on that rooftop, regret washed over him. When he tried to sleep, his bed must have reminded him of his adultery. When he sat at the table and looked at the place Uriah had occupied during that dinner marked with hypocrisy, his appetite probably disappeared. When he was dealing with the affairs of state and tried to write, no doubt the letter with the instructions to kill Uriah came to his memory.

Worst of all, David had lost the joy of communion with God.

All sin is against God

When the prophet Nathan charged King David with what he had done, he asked: *"Why did you despise the word of the Lord?"* God, speaking through His prophet, said, *"You despised me."* Nathan went on to say, *"You have shown utter contempt for the Lord."* (2 Samuel 12:9, 10, 14) David responded to the prophet by saying, *"I have sinned against the Lord."* (2 Samuel 12:13)

David's horrible crimes—rape, deception, murder—tragically affected their immediate victims, Bathsheba and Uriah. But all sin is, first and foremost, against God, against His law and against His will. Thus, in his confession and petition to God, David said, *"Against you, you only, have I sinned and done what is evil in your sight; so you are right in your verdict and justified when you judge."* (Psalm 51:4) David was saying that whatever God does, He has more than enough reasons to do it, and He does it in a perfectly righteous way.

This helps to explain why, when *sins* are the problem, Jesus teaches us to ask the Father to forgive our *debts*. (Actually, the version of the Lord's Prayer presented in Luke's Gospel says, *"Forgive us our sins.)* When we sin, we sin against God Himself, which imposes an obligation on us that we can't possibly fulfill on our own, a burden that we can't get rid of at will, a debt we will never be able to settle.

Given what David did to Bathsheba and Uriah, it's difficult to understand why God described him as *"a man after his own heart"* (1 Samuel 13:14). But an examination of David's prayers helps to explain it.

Have mercy on me, O God, according to your unfailing love; according to your great compassion blot out my transgressions. Wash away all my iniquity and cleanse me from my sin. For I know my transgressions, and my sin is always before me. ...

Cleanse me with hyssop, and I will be clean; wash me, and I will be whiter than snow. Let me hear joy and gladness; let the bones you have crushed rejoice. Hide your face from my sins and blot out all my iniquity. Create in me a pure heart, O God, and renew a steadfast spirit within me. Do not cast me from your presence or take Your Holy Spirit from me. Restore to me the joy of your salvation and grant me a willing spirit, to sustain me. (Psalm 51:1–3, 7–12)

David lived with an awareness that sin not only violates God's commandments but also gets in the way of a relationship with God. And so he prayed, *"Search me, O God, and know my heart; test me and know my thoughts. See if there is any wicked way in me, and lead me in the way everlasting."* (Psalm 139:23–24 *NRSV*)

God forgives sin

David's sin had tragic consequences, not only for Bathsheba and Uriah, but in his own life as well. The prophecies of Nathan were fulfilled: the son born to Bathsheba died shortly after his birth; years later, another son would rebel, attempting to take the kingdom away from David and sleeping with some of his father's wives—on the roof of the palace! But that day when Nathan prophesied God's judgment, he said something more to David: *"The Lord has taken away your sin."* (2 Samuel 12:13)

Did David deserve God's mercy? Surely not. David's sins were unimaginably wicked, especially for a man who had been appointed a servant of God. But God forgave him. The question of whether we deserve God's forgiveness is settled: we do not. God's forgiveness is a sovereign act; He is under no obligation to forgive us. God forgives because He wants to forgive. The Apostle Paul writes: *"For by grace you have been saved through faith, and this is not your own doing; it is the gift of God—not the result of works, so that no one may boast."* (Ephesians 2:8–9 *NRSV*)

In a certain sense, though, God's forgiveness does depend on us. David was forgiven because he confessed his sin. He wrote, *"I acknowledged my sin to you and did not cover up my iniquity. I said, 'I will confess my transgressions to the Lord.' And you forgave the guilt of my sin."* (Psalm 32:5) God's forgiveness depends on our confession. *"If we confess our sins, he who is faithful and just will forgive us our sins and cleanse us from all unrighteousness."* (1 John 1:9 *NRSV*)

Beyond the confession of our sins, the Lord seeks for a change of attitude and action on our part. David described sorrow for sin as *"a broken and contrite heart"* (Psalm 51:17). But feeling a sense of guilt and shame is not repentance. Repentance means turning away from sin to live in a way that pleases God. *"Let the wicked forsake their ways and the unrighteous their thoughts. Let them turn to the Lord, and he will have mercy on them, and to our God, for he will freely pardon."* (Isaiah 55:7)

God spoke of His justice and mercy—and repentance—through His prophet Ezekiel:

If a righteous person turns from their righteousness and commits sin, they will die for it; because of the sin they have committed they will die. But if a wicked person turns away from the wickedness they have committed and does what is just and right, they will save their life. Because they consider all the offenses they have committed and turn away from them, that person will surely live; they will not die. (Ezekiel 18:26–28).

This passage is a call to repentance, but it is also a reminder that the penalty for sin is death. David recognized that his sin separated him from God. That's what sin does. It makes a relationship with God impossible. If we persist in sin and do not deal with it as we should, our sin will lead to *eternal* separation from God. *"For the wages of sin is death ... "* (Romans 6:23a); but God forgives: *"... the gift of God is eternal life in Christ Jesus our Lord."* (Romans 6:23b) If we confess our sin and turn from our wicked way to God's way, claiming the gift of salvation available to us because of the sacrifice of Christ on Calvary, we are forgiven, and eternal life is ours.

That's one more reason why it helps us to think of our sins as debts we owe to God. Jesus paid the penalty for our sins with His death on the Cross. That's a debt we can never repay. So we must pray, "Forgive us our debts."

God's forgiveness is unlimited

The forgiveness of God is not subject to any prerequisites. Beyond confession and repentance, there is nothing we need do to receive it.

Many people don't experience forgiveness because they haven't asked for it. They may say: "What I did is unforgivable. I don't think God can forgive me." Or "I'm just not worthy of God's forgiveness." Or "I've asked God for forgiveness so many times that I'm ashamed to go back and do it again."

Such thoughts come from Satan, the deceiver. The promise of God is straightforward, with no restrictions: *"If we confess our sins, he who is faithful and just will forgive us our sins and cleanse us from all unrighteousness."* (1 John 1:9 *NRSV)*

Others find it hard to believe that they truly have *been* forgiven. Memories of past sins haunt them, and they are plagued with feelings of condemnation. Again, this is a trick of the enemy. God's forgiveness is complete. This was the experience of David the psalmist: *"Blessed is the one whose transgressions are forgiven, whose sins are covered. Blessed is the one whose sin the Lord does not count against them."* (Psalm 32:1–2) The moment we are forgiven, the balance of our sins in God's register of accounts becomes zero. What has been settled is settled! God says, *"I will forgive their wickedness and will remember their sins no more."* (Jeremiah 31:34)

For a believer to live with unconfessed sin is tragic. Many people struggle with insomnia and even depression because they carry such a burden. Medications may offer temporarily relief from their sufferings but cannot provide a cure. As long as these people resist turning humbly to God, they delay the restorative process. As part of his confession, David prayed, *"Restore to me the joy of your salvation."* (Psalm 51:12) That's what God's forgiveness will do.

Unconfessed sin is also a hindrance to prayer. That thing in us that is unpleasing to God will restrict our access to Him. Our prayers will not receive the answering echo to which we are accustomed; rather, heaven will seem like a vault of brass. But when we confess our sins to the Father, when we ask Him for forgiveness, we experience the removal of every obstacle that might otherwise prevent us from having perfect communion with Him. His forgiveness is the path to full, complete happiness.

What about you?

Is your prayer life unfruitful? Do you feel that you are not being heard? If so, is it possible that some sin in your life is blocking the way? Don't hesitate to turn to your heavenly Father in confession and repentance and offer your humble petition: "Forgive me my debts. Forgive my sins."

Sorrow for your sin will not bring relief, but God's forgiveness will bring total liberation. He invites you—He invites all of us—with these words:

> 'Turn to me now, while there is time. Give me your hearts. Come with fasting, weeping, and mourning. Don't tear your clothing in your grief, but tear your hearts instead.' Return to the Lord your God, for he is merciful and compassionate, slow to get angry and filled with unfailing love. He is eager to relent and not punish. (Joel 2:12–13 NLT)

Let us pray...

Heavenly Father, I praise you for your great love.
Thank you that when I sin, you don't want to condemn me, but rather to restore me. I acknowledge
that this is possible only through your grace. Now I
come to you, confessing my failures and asking you to
forgive my sins and guide me along the path of your
will. O compassionate God, show me your love again,
and I will testify to others about what you have done
for me. I ask this in the name of Jesus Christ.

Amen

9

"As we forgive our debtors"

Be merciful toward those who have wronged you

JESUS' TEACHING CHALLENGED THE CULTURE of His own time and place—as it has continued to challenge every culture in the centuries since, all around the world. He shocked those who heard Him, including His disciples, when He insisted that the traditional rules of behavior that they had been taught just weren't good enough, particularly when it came to how people should treat one another. He said things like, *"Love your enemies, do good to those who hate you, bless those who curse you, pray for those who mistreat you."* (Luke 6:27–28) And Jesus talked a lot about forgiveness.

According to an ancient tradition of the Jewish rabbis, someone who had been wronged was obligated to forgive, not just the first time around, but when the offense was committed a second and even a third time. If the offense was repeated a fourth time, however, no forgiveness was required. In fact, the person who had been wronged was then free to follow the principle set forth in the Old Testament Law: *"eye for eye, tooth for tooth"* (Exodus 21:23–25). That meant that if one person hurt another in some way, the one who was hurt could do the same thing in return— but no more. (If I knock out one of your teeth, you can knock out one of mine—but not all of them!) It was essentially, "Do to others as they do to you." Jesus, on the other hand, said, *"Do to others as you would have them do to you."* (Luke 6:31)

Peter thought the Master must have His own rule about how far a person has to go in forgiving others. Three times probably wouldn't be enough. So *"Peter came to Jesus and asked, 'Lord, how many times shall I forgive my brother or sister who sins against me? Up to seven times?' Jesus answered, 'I tell you, not seven times, but seventy-seven times.'"* (Matthew 18:21–22) The Savior's response illustrates the truth of God's word spoken through His prophet hundreds of years before:

> *'For my thoughts are not your thoughts, neither are your ways my ways,' declares the Lord. 'As the heavens are higher than the earth, so are my ways higher than your ways and my thoughts than your thoughts.' (Isaiah 55:8–9)*

An unpayable debt

Then Jesus told a story to emphasize His point: our forgiveness of others should be like God's forgiveness of us—unlimited.

> *'The kingdom of heaven is like a certain king who wanted to settle accounts with his servants. And when he had begun to settle accounts, one was brought to him who owed him ten thousand talents. But as he was not able to pay, his master commanded that he be sold, with his wife and children and all that he had, and that payment be made.' (Matthew 18:23–25 NKJV)*

We are given no information as to how this servant incurred his debt, but it was immense: 10,000 talents of silver. A talent was a monetary measure of about 56 pounds in weight; so the servant owed the king the equivalent of roughly 280 tons of silver, which on today's money market amounts to more than $140 million.

Clearly, the servant was in deep trouble, unable to repay such an enormous debt. Nevertheless, the king demanded payment. When the servant could not pay, the king ordered that he be sold along with his wife and children and all his property. That way, the king would recoup at least some of his money.

Have you ever felt the burden of a debt you couldn't pay? Perhaps you're one of those few people who don't believe in carrying financial debt. But these days, most of us can't buy much or do much without a credit card of some kind; only the comparatively wealthy can buy real estate without having to shoulder a mortgage.

It's all too easy too easy to get into a position in which it is impossible to pay off debts. Sometimes this occurs due to changed circumstances, such as sudden unemployment or poor health. A person might say, "I had to take out a big loan, because if I didn't, I would have lost my house." Some people may get carried away by an impulse and make a large spur–of–the–moment purchase: "I just felt like I had to have that car—I couldn't resist!" Others fall into debt seeking pleasures of various kinds. There are also those who end up in debt because of ignorance. They sing loan documents without first reading the terms and conditions, only to plead later, "I didn't know what I was signing."

On a whole different scale, consider the national debt of the United States. According to the Treasury Department, in September 2005 it was roughly $8 trillion. By September 2015, it had increased to 18 trillion: $18,000,000,000,000. And it is growing at an accelerated rate.

Economist Paul Kasriel, representing the Northern Trust Corporation, a financial services firm, said that "the U.S. debt will not be paid by those who now have jobs, not even by those who are currently breathing. The debt will be transferred to the next generation ... and the next."[1] In other words, this is an unpayable debt.

But debts such as these, whether on the personal or the national level, pale by comparison with the debt faced by everyone on earth. The king in Jesus' story represents God, the ultimate judge. The servant represents humankind, helpless under the weight of the unpayable debt of sin.

A gracious king
But Jesus' story doesn't end there. It goes on:

> 'The servant therefore fell down before him, saying, "Master, have patience with me, and I will pay you all." Then the master of that servant was moved with compassion, released him, and forgave him the debt.' (Matthew 18:26–27 NKJV)

The servant humbled himself, falling prostrate at the feet of the king and asking for patience; he promised that he would eventually pay all that he owed. The king knew better. He knew the servant would never be able to amass such a sum. But he was "moved with compassion," and in an act of grace, he forgave the debt.

"Each of us will give an account of ourselves to God." (Romans

---

1   The quotation appears in an article by Bill Bonner on the website: www.lewrockwell.com.

14:12) When we are called before our Judge, all our past promises to be good will mean nothing. Our family connections or religious traditions will have no value. Attempts to place the blame on others for our mistakes or to point to our good works—all our arguments, justifications, and excuses—will not serve to achieve a balance in our favor. Sin is a debt that even the most extreme personal sacrifice could never pay.

With one exception: the perfect sacrifice of Christ on the Cross of Calvary. *"God made him who had no sin to be sin for us, so that in him we might become the righteousness of God."* (2 Corinthians 5:21)

The grace, the undeserved mercy, we receive from God frees us from the judgment to which sin condemns us. *"There is now no condemnation for those who are in Christ Jesus."* (Romans 8:1) The judgment of the king in the story Jesus told was that the servant and his family be sold to pay the debt. We were not sold, but *"were bought, not with something that ruins like gold or silver, but with the precious blood of Christ, who was like a pure and perfect lamb."* (1 Peter 1:18–19 *NCV)*

God covered over our great debt with a greater mercy. The death of Jesus on the Cross declares the endless love of God, which forgives all our sins.

From time to time we need to have the memory of God's saving love brought fresh before our eyes. We need to be reminded of where the Lord found us and where He has taken us.

> *I waited patiently for the Lord; he turned to me and heard my cry. He lifted me out of the slimy pit, out of the mud and mire; he set my feet on a rock and gave me a firm place to stand. He put a new song in my mouth, a hymn of praise to our God. (Psalm 40:1–3)*

An ungrateful servant

Sadly, there is more to the story Jesus told:

> 'But that servant went out and found one of his fellow
> servants who owed him a hundred denarii; and he laid
> hands on him and took him by the throat, saying, "Pay
> me what you owe!" So his fellow servant fell down at his
> feet and begged him, saying, "Have patience with me,
> and I will pay you all." And he would not, but went and
> threw him into prison till he should pay the debt.' (Mat-
> thew 18:28–30 NKJV)

As the third scene in this drama opens, the servant who has just walked out of the king's presence free of his enormous debt goes looking for someone who owes him a much, much smaller amount: 100 denarii, about a pound of silver—worth just over $250 in today's market. Servant No. 1 grabs hold of Servant No. 2 and demands payment. Servant No. 2 can't repay the debt, so he makes a request of Servant No. 1—exactly the same request Servant No. 1 had made of the king: "Give me some time, and I'll pay up." But Servant No. 1 refuses. He goes to the authorities and accuses Servant No. 2 of fraud, demanding that he be put in jail.

What a horrible man! It would never occur to you or me to do something like he did. Or would it?

We come before God loaded down with sin, unable to re-deem ourselves, morally and spiritually bankrupt. Moved with compassion, our heavenly Father forgives our debt, setting us free to start over, to live in a way that pleases Him. Then someone hurts our feelings, betrays our trust, takes advantage of our loy-alty, or simply insults us, and the old nature that we were sure was dead, buried, and forgotten shakes off the dust of the grave and rises up. Suddenly we want to collect everything we are owed, to the penny. Thoughts of patience and mercy burn off like morning fog in the heat of the day. We want an indebted head to roll. At the very least, we want to humiliate the offender—better yet, to "do to the other as the other has done to us."

The Bible warns us against such feelings of resentment: "Watch out that no poisonous root of bitterness grows up to trouble you." (Hebrews 12:15 NLT) A root of bitterness chokes out the fruit of the Spirit; instead, we reap irritation, annoyance, vexation, setback, distaste, disgust, anger, pain, suffering, agony, grief. As a result, our relationships with God and our neighbors are sorely affected.

Our natural ability to forgive is very limited. It hurts to forgive. When I was about 14, I started having problems with one of my molars. I was terrified of going to the dentist. (I still am!) So I took a painkiller, but the problem persisted. The swelling increased and the pain got worse—but I did not want to face the dentist. Finally I did, and the pain was gone forever … along with the tooth.

My resistance to going to the dentist—and the pain that built up—is like our resistance to forgiving others, and the infectious sore that eats away at our hearts because we are just too proud to do what we know could heal us. Charles Stanley observes, "Whatever your situation, whatever has happened in your past, remember that you are the loser if you do not deal with an unforgiving spirit. And the people around you suffer too."[2]

When we don't forgive, we're just like Servant No. 1, the

---

2   Charles Stanley, *The Gift of Forgiveness* (Thomas Nelson, 1991).

wicked man of the story. That is an affront to our Father, who has forgiven us all the wrong we have done.

A severe punishment

The last part of Jesus' story tells what happened as a result of the actions of the ungrateful servant:

> 'So when his fellow servants saw what had been done, they were very grieved, and came and told their master all that had been done. Then his master, after he had called him, said to him, "You wicked servant! I forgave you all that debt because you begged me. Should you not also have had compassion on your fellow servant, just as I had pity on you?" And his master was angry, and delivered him to the torturers until he should pay all that was due to him.' (Matthew 18:31–34 NKJV)

The king soon learned what the servant had done. Though we might act as if everything is going along as usual, when we take revenge on one who has offended us, God knows it. If we harbor any hidden resentment, God knows it. Our hearts are an open book to Him. King David was well aware of this.

> If I say, 'Surely the darkness will hide me and the light become night around me,' even the darkness will not be dark to you; the night will shine like the day, for darkness is as light to you. (Psalm 139:11–12)

When the wicked servant was called back to the king, there was no one to intercede for him. His arguments, pleading, and crying were to no avail. This time there was no mercy. Jesus said, *"The measure you use will be the measure you receive."* (Luke 6:38 *NET*)

The king's charge against the servant essentially was this: "You should have used the same measure toward your fellow servant as I used toward you." His exact words were, *"Should you not also have had compassion on your fellow servant, just as I had pity on you?"* The word "pity" in this verse literally means, "Feeling sympathy for another person in misery, and especially sympathy manifested in deeds;"[3] it is to be merciful toward the needy. Actually, in the original Greek text, the same word is used for both "compassion" and "pity," and is more literally translated "mercy."

What did this servant lose because he failed to be merciful? He did not receive mercy; he lost all his possessions—and his wife and children—and was eventually thrown into prison. He must have felt a terrible burden of guilt and grief.

At the end of His story, after Jesus told how the king punished the ungrateful servant, He said, *"So my heavenly Father will also do to every one of you, if you do not forgive your brother or sister from your heart."* (Matthew 18:35 *NRSV*)

When we don't forgive those who sin against us, our relationship with our heavenly Father quickly shrivels up and our relationships with others grow cold. Before we know it, *"love, joy, peace, patience, kindness, generosity, faithfulness, gentleness, and self–control"* (Galatians 5:22–23 *NRSV*) will be gone. No ritual, no charity, no mission offering, no commitment, no sacrifice will remedy this loss.

However, the ultimate loss that results from failing to forgive

---

3   W.E. Vine, *Vine's Expository Dictionary* (Thomas Nelson, 1999).

others is eternal. Immediately after giving His disciples a model for prayer, Jesus said to them: *"For if you forgive other people when they sin against you, your heavenly Father will also forgive you. But if you do not forgive others their sins, your Father will not forgive your sins."* (Matthew 6:14–15) Only the merciful will be shown mercy. (Matthew 5:7)

James adds this solemn warning: *"Judgment without mercy will be shown to anyone who has not been merciful. Mercy triumphs over judgment."* (James 2:13)

A chain of mercy

Jesus said to His disciples, and He says to us: *"Freely you have received; freely give."* (Matthew 10:8) When we are recipients of God's mercy, we immediately acquire a moral obligation of very large dimensions, which we cannot ignore. Max Lucado writes:

> If God can tolerate my mistakes, can't I tolerate the mistakes of others? If God can overlook my errors, can't I overlook the errors of others? If God allows me with my foibles and failures to call him Father, shouldn't I extend the same grace to others?[4]

Sometimes the people we find it hardest to forgive are fellow Christians. After all, we expect more from them than from unbelievers. Nevertheless, we cannot have complete forgiveness from God until we have forgiven those who have offended us. The Apostle Paul urges, *"Bear with one another and, if anyone has a complaint against another, forgive each other; just as the Lord has forgiven you, so you also must forgive."* (Colossians 3:13 *NRSV*)

---

4 Max Lucado, *When God Whispers Your Name* (Thomas Nelson, 1999).

There are unparalleled riches awaiting the one who learns to forgive. Some years ago, I visited the southern part of Venezuela, a region where mineral riches abound. In a village, I met a miner. As we talked, the man took a small vial from his pocket; inside it was a piece of gold. That tiny bit of metal represented a priceless commodity. The area around the mines was wild; animals and humans alike were disease–ridden, and criminals lurked about. Yet many adventurers penetrated the region, sometimes staying for months, with one objective in mind: to find gold. Discovering a vein would mean having enough money to buy whatever they thought would bring them pleasure. Many treasure–seekers died in their quest; yet when someone struck gold, all would agree, "It was worth it!"

In one of His many parables about the kingdom of heaven, Jesus spoke about finding a treasure hidden in a field and selling everything to buy the field that contained the treasure. (Matthew 13:44) Someone who has been hurt by another might say, "I can't find it in my heart to forgive." Forgiving isn't easy; it may present great challenges. But it's worth it to dig for that treasure! Finding the precious ore of forgiveness toward others yields *"an inexpressible and glorious joy"* (1 Peter 1:8) and peace *"that surpasses all understanding"* (Philippians 4:7 *NET)*. And when we find that place of forgiveness, there is a party in heaven; Father, Son, and Spirit join the angels in rejoicing.

The wounds that have been opened by an offense can often be closed up and healed by forgiveness. For this to happen, an attitude of forgiveness must become an action of forgiveness. A decision to forgive must be accompanied by an effort at reconciliation. Jesus said:

'When you are offering your gift at the altar, if you re-member that your brother or sister has something against you, leave your gift there before the altar and go; first be reconciled to your brother or sister, and then come and offer your gift.' (Matthew 5:23–24 NRSV)

One of the greatest blessings that come with a forgiving spirit is the restoration of an unhindered relationship with God, which clears the way for prayer. When we have settled our accounts with God and our neighbor, we are free to enjoy this glorious privilege, to tend to this most sacred ministry. Jesus declared: *"When you stand praying, if you hold anything against anyone, forgive them, so that your Father in heaven may forgive you your sins."* (Mark 11:25)

The principle and the practice are really quite simple: *"Be merciful, just as your Father is merciful."* (Luke 6:36) He forgave—and continues to forgive—my sins against Him. So I must in turn forgive those who sin against me. If I don't do that, the process comes to a halt; the system breaks down. If I am not forgiving, I am not forgiven. But when I do forgive, I have the assurance of the unlimited mercy of a loving Father.

What about you?

Have you been offended to such a degree, and suffered so much, that you feel you cannot forgive? Do you feel that this grievance is the straw that broke the camel's back? Do you think someone owes you an apology? This may seem perfectly reasonable, from a human standpoint. But, remember, your heavenly Father's way of thinking is not like yours. (Isaiah 55:8–9) The forgiveness you have received should compel you to do the same for those who are indebted to you.

Before you say your next prayer, ask yourself if you have a grudge against someone; if so, make the decision to forgive. This act will release God's providence upon you.

Forgive, and barriers of hatred will be replaced by bridges of love. Forgive, and dark indifference will be replaced by the bright fires of compassion. Forgive, and stormy gales of trouble will become balmy winds of grace.

Let us pray ...

Heavenly Father, with all my heart I thank you that you have forgiven me. Because of the unlimited riches of your grace, I can stand before you. Your Word is clear when it says I should forgive those who have offended me, in the same way as you have forgiven me. Help me to obey your Word. I don't want my prayers to be hampered. Engender in me the courage to make decisions that are just and right. Lord, do not let me forget what you have done for me. Help me to become an example to others of humility and compassion.

Amen

10

"Lead us not into temptation"

Resist the devil's enticements

IN JUNE 2007, I WENT to Haltom City, Texas, a suburb of Fort Worth, as part of a Salvation Army disaster relief team. A river had overflowed and flooded part of the city. Several homes were washed away and many others badly damaged. In all, more than 100 homes were affected.

White Branch Creek was a narrow stream that for many years had not given local residents any cause for concern. Even that June, high–water emergencies in nearby towns did not alarm Haltom City authorities; no evacuation orders were issued. However, a combination of torrential rain and upstream flooding caused the creek to overflow. The rushing water hit hard, and many of the townspeople were living in mobile homes, which were not built to withstand that level of flooding. Most of those homes had no solid base, no foundation; typically, the structure rested on a few bricks or a flatbed trailer.

Many believers are like those mobile homes; their faith and obedience to God are swept away for lack of a firm foundation. Their resistance to temptation gives way in the storms of life.

Jesus said:

> *'Anyone who listens to my teaching and follows it is wise,*
> *like a person who builds a house on solid rock. Though*
> *the rain comes in torrents and the floodwaters rise and*
> *the winds beat against that house, it won't collapse*
> *because it is built on bedrock. But anyone who hears my*
> *teaching and doesn't obey it is foolish, like a person who*
> *builds a house on sand. When the rains and floods come*
> *and the winds beat against that house, it will collapse*
> *with a mighty crash.' (Matthew 7:24–27 NLT)*

Storms of temptation come into the life of every believer. The best "home insurance" we can have at such times is a life founded on God's Word.

We are all tempted in different ways. Some of us have a tendency to be materialistic—to want things, whether we need them or not. Some of us are inclined to be proud or self–centered. Some are vulnerable to sexual sins. Others are quick to criticize or to be envious. The challenge for many is failing to tell the truth.

Analysis of just about any given temptation will show that it is related to one of three types of human impulses or motivations:

1) Natural appetites—such as for food, drink, and sexual intimacy.

2) A desire for things of this world, both material, such as a comfortable home and fashionable clothes; and social, such as the respect and admiration of others.

3) A desire to feel good about ourselves and to be successful.

None of these is sinful in itself. God created us with physical appetites, an appreciation for beauty and comfort, a need for positive social connections, and the impetus to be and do our best. But each of them contains the potential for sin, mostly when carried to excess. In his first epistle, the Apostle John described what that looks like: (1) *"a craving for physical pleasure"*; (2) *"a craving for everything we see"*; (3) *"pride in our achievements and posessions"* (1 John 2:16 *NLT*).

The Scriptures say that during His time on earth, Jesus was *"tempted in every way, just as we are—yet he did not sin."* (Hebrews 4:15) This should be a great encouragement to us. Because Jesus faced temptation, He understands what we're going through when we face temptation—and He can help us resist it. (Hebrews 2:18) And the fact that Jesus didn't sin when He was tempted tells us that it's possible for us to resist temptation if we follow His example. In fact, the best way to learn how to resist temptation is by looking at how Jesus did it.

A vulnerable target

Jesus had just had a "mountaintop experience." He had traveled from Galilee down to the spot on the Jordan River where John was preaching repentance and baptizing those who responded. Immediately after Jesus Himself had been baptized, as He was coming out of the water, the sky opened up and the Holy Spirit, in the form of a dove, flew down and rested on Him. Then His Father spoke out of heaven, saying, *"This is my Son, whom I love; with him I am well pleased."* (Matthew 3:17) This affirmation of Jesus' position and ministry must have filled Him with great joy. It also helped to prepare Him for the ordeal to come.

Mountaintop experiences are often followed by formidable temptations. There is nothing the devil enjoys more than bringing us down to defeat—which is always his purpose in tempting us. On the other hand, meeting with God helps to make us ready to resist temptation.

Jesus was prepared to face temptation because He was in constant communication with His Father and because His knowledge of God's Word was both broad and deep. And when temptation came, He relied on the power and wisdom of the Holy Spirit for protection.

> *Then Jesus was led up by the Spirit into the wilderness to be tempted by the devil. He fasted forty days and forty nights, and afterwards he was famished. The tempter came and said to him, 'If you are the Son of God, command these stones to become loaves of bread.' But he answered, 'It is written, "One does not live by bread alone, but by every word that comes from the mouth of God."'*
> (Matthew 4:1–4 NRSV)

Picture Jesus at the beginning of those 40 days in the wilderness—strong, full of energy and vitality. The second day, He would have begun to feel hunger pangs, and possibly have a slight headache. During the day, the desert heat would have been almost unbearable, and perspiration would have made Him lose bodily fluid. At night, the temperature would have plunged, and He would have felt the bitter cold acutely, particularly in His hands and feet. Day by day, the physical effects of a lack of food would have been more and more extreme.

One of the first symptoms experienced by someone who fasts

for an extended period is dehydration; then, because food intake has ceased, the stores of minerals in the body become exhausted. Fatigue sets in, accompanied by dry mouth, nausea, and a progressive decrease in muscle strength. No doubt Jesus began to lose weight; His legs trembled with weakness; and He felt His heart beating much more rapidly. Because fasting tends to cause insomnia, He probably got little sleep.

By the end of 40 days, Jesus' appearance would have changed dramatically: sunken eyes, a languid face, skin that seemed stuck to the underlying bones, thin arms and legs. His body would have used up all possible energy reserves. He would have been physically weak and very, very hungry.

A cunning adversary

The predator stalks its prey, watching and waiting for just the right moment of vulnerability. When the prey is careless, wounded, or weak from hunger or thirst, the predator will attack without mercy. *"The devil prowls around like a roaring lion looking for someone to devour."* (1 Peter 5:8) So it is not surprising that just at the moment when Jesus was at His most vulnerable, the devil showed up to entice and cajole Him to disobey His Father. Jesus was an authentic man in a desperate situation: far from human society, in an arid, lifeless environment, and weak with hunger. And the predator pounced: *"If you are the Son of God, command these stones to become loaves of bread."* Extreme need creates susceptibility to temptation.

Under these circumstances, who would blame Jesus if He used some of His power in this way? Didn't He need food? Didn't He have a right to it? After all, He was the Son of God! But Jesus knew better. He knew that no suggestion, no urging from Satan could possibly be good. So, prompted by the Holy Spirit, Jesus drew from His knowledge of the Scriptures to rebuff His enemy. He quoted the ancient book of Deuteronomy: *"One does not live by bread alone, but by every word that comes from the mouth of the Lord."* (Deuteronomy 8:3 *NRSV*) Jesus was saying, in effect, "I'm not about to listen to you, Satan. I listen to what my Father says; that's more valuable to me than food."

We live in a time in which the voice of God can easily become faint as we hear the voice of the devil on every side. His voice is not always loud and raucous. The book of Proverbs describes a beautiful woman attempting to persuade a young man to make love to her:

> *"With persuasive words she led him astray; she seduced him with her smooth talk. All at once he followed her like an ox going to the slaughter, like a deer stepping into a noose till an arrow pierces his liver, like a bird darting into a snare, little knowing it will cost him his life."*
> *(Proverbs 7:21–23)*

Television, movies, and social media have used "smooth talk" to make believers think that dishonesty, cruelty, and debauchery are "not that bad." After all, no one wants to be thought intolerant or small-minded. Unfortunately, the path that leads from no longer disapproving of behavior to approving of it to practicing it can be surprisingly short.

An even more subtle form of temptation is Satan's reminding us of our physical needs in order to cause us to neglect time spent alone with God in prayer and reading the Bible. In the evening, the devil whispers softly in our ear: "You're too tired right now. You can always do your devotions in the morning." When morning comes, his message is, "Wait until you're more wide awake. You want to give your best time to Bible reading and prayer." Hunger, thirst, even a need for physical exercise can come to seem more important—at the moment—than time with our Father. In the end, we become prey in the jaws of the most deadly of predators.

If we are to deal effectively with temptation, we must do what Jesus did. He was in constant contact with His Father, often praying through the night. He absorbed God's Word and allowed it to absorb Him, because He was persuaded that it was the source of truth and life. And He was at all times looking to the Holy Spirit for wisdom and power.

An appeal to pride

When Satan tried to persuade Jesus to turn those stones into bread, he was doing more than taking advantage of His hunger. The devil was trying to play on Jesus' self–esteem by tempting Him to display pride. Satan challenged Jesus' position, saying, *"If* you are the Son of God." The natural response would have been egotistical: *"Of course* I'm the Son of God! Not long ago, my Father acknowledged me, crying from heaven: 'This is my Son, whom I love.' " By implication, the devil was saying: "OK. Prove it by turning these stones into bread."

This very much resembles the temptation of Adam and Eve in the Garden of Eden. Satan appealed not only to Eve's desire for something delicious to eat but also to her ego. After all, the garden was full of trees laden with luscious fruit of all kinds. But when the devil tempted Eve to eat fruit from the forbidden tree of the knowledge of good and evil, he said to her, " *'For God knows that when you eat from it your eyes will be opened, and you will be like God, knowing good and evil.'* " (Genesis 3:5) Tragically, Eve's pride rose up, and she chose to believe Satan rather than God. *"When the woman saw that the fruit of the tree was good for food and pleasing to the eye,* and also desirable for gaining wisdom, *she took some and ate it. She also gave some to her husband, who was with her, and he ate it."* (Genesis 3:6)

When personal pride sets itself up against what God has said, it can only be called arrogance. Arrogance is a kind of self-worship. Arrogant people have an exaggerated idea of their own worth and importance and, in particular, often think they are smarter than anyone else, and they don't hesitate to let others know it. Unfortunately, the vanity of the arrogant quickly overrides good judgment. *"Pride goes before destruction and a haughty spirit before a fall."* (Proverbs 16:18)

But Jesus knew that when the Father says something, He means what He says. No arguments or demonstrations are required to prove that His word is true. So Jesus refused to give in to Satan's appeal to His pride. His response, in essence, was, "I live by what God says." That allegiance was infinitely more important to Him than any feelings He might have about Himself.

A challenge to God's word

The devil doesn't give up easily. When one of his tactics doesn't work, he will try another one. If he finds someone who would rather listen to God than pursue satisfaction of physical needs and desires, someone who subordinates self and lifts up the heavenly Father, Satan may attack that person's faith.

The devil knows the Bible well and interprets it according to his own convenience. He may have thought: "So you want to play sanctimonious with me? I'll attack you with the same weapon you're using to defend yourself: Scripture." So he challenged Jesus again, and this time his approach was more subtle, camouflaged with an Old Testament promise.

> *Then the devil took him to the holy city and placed him on the pinnacle of the temple, saying to him, 'If you are the Son of God, throw yourself down; for it is written, "He will command his angels concerning you," and "On their hands they will bear you up, so that you will not dash your foot against a stone."' Jesus said to him, 'Again it is written, "Do not put the Lord your God to the test."' (Matthew 4:5–7 NRSV)*

It's amazing how Satan uses God's words as a tool to confuse and persuade. In his dialogue with Eve, he began by misquoting what God had said: " *'Did God really say, "You must not eat from any tree in the garden"?'* " (Genesis 3:1) Eve corrected him, telling him that God had said she and Adam could eat fruit from any tree in the garden except one—the tree of knowledge of good and evil—but that God had also said that if they did eat from that forbidden tree, they would die. Satan then directly contradicted what God had said: "*'You will* not *certainly die.'*" (Genesis 3:4) The devil's purpose was to create confusion, then incite disobedience.

Now, with Jesus, Satan uses the same tactics. He quotes from two verses of Psalm 91 (11, 12) that promise God's protection to those who trust in Him. The devil is implying that if this promise applies to anyone, it surely must apply to Jesus—*if* He is the Son of God. Satan is saying something like this: "Try and see if God is really with you. See if He will keep His word. If He is indeed your Father, He will have to save you … right?" What is at stake here is God's credibility. Will He fulfill His promises? Can He really be trusted?

Jesus offers no arguments. He makes it clear that He has no intention of discussing the meaning of these two lines of Scripture, taken out of context. He unhesitatingly responds to the tempter, quoting Deuteronomy 6:16: *"'Again it is written, "Do not put the Lord your God to the test." ' "*

If the devil can't distract us from reading the Bible, he will do everything he can to make us doubt it, to wonder whether what God says is really true. The key to successfully overcoming temptation is to recognize that God will keep His word—without our having to test Him.

When someone quotes Scripture, especially to persuade believers to do something—or not to do something—it is incumbent on them to be sure that the Scripture is being used rightly. As a result of being fooled by the misuse of Scripture, many believers have been knocked down and have fallen away; churches have been divided; and servants of God have left the work.

An offer of power

The devil hadn't finished with Jesus. This time, he confronted Him with a temptation that is almost irresistible to most humans: power, glory, and wealth.

> *Again, the devil took him to a very high mountain and showed him all the kingdoms of the world and their splendor; and he said to him, 'All these I will give you,*

if you will fall down and worship me.' (Matthew 4:8–9 NRSV)

To become the perfect sacrifice for the sin of the world, the Son of God had *"emptied himself … being born in human likeness … being found in human form."* (Philippians 2:7–8 *NRSV*) Now Jesus was at His lowest ebb as a human being. After 40 days of fasting, He must have felt utterly alone, depleted in body and spirit, like the poorest man on earth. What could be a more effective temptation than an offer to take Him out of anonymity and misery?

On the other hand, the day would come when *"at the name of Jesus every knee [would] bow—in heaven, on earth, and under the earth."* (Philippians 2:10 *NET*) In days long past, the eternal Father had declared: *"You are my son; today I have become your father. Ask me, and I will make the nations your inheritance, the ends of the earth your possession."* (Psalm 2:7–8)

The devil knew all this and was determined to nip any such plan in the bud. His own cherished ambition was—and is—to be recognized and worshiped as a god. He was offering Jesus the position of vice–regent, a kind of secondary king serving under the rule of the real king: Satan himself. Jesus knew that the devil was "the prince of this world"; much of humanity was in fact in bondage to him. But the prince of this world had *"no hold over"* Jesus, he *"stood condemned,"* and he would soon *"be driven out."* (John 14:30; 16:11; 12:31) Jesus had no need to be rewarded by the devil with what the Father had already promised Him.

In addition to power and glory, Satan was offering Jesus the wealth of the world. This is one of the most dangerous areas for Christians. The Apostle Paul warned Timothy about it:

Those who want to get rich fall into temptation and a trap and into many foolish and harmful desires that plunge people into ruin and destruction. For the love of money is a root of all kinds of evil. Some people, eager for money, have wandered from the faith and pierced themselves with many griefs. (1 Timothy 6:9–10)

By deceiving people into mistaking wants for needs, Satan makes the pursuit of wealth look acceptable and even commendable. But God has promised to supply all our needs. (Philippians 4:19) The devil wants to persuade us to seek from him what God has already promised us. All he asks of is a gesture, just a *little* worship—ultimately, however, that we declare him god, in place of our Father. The offer may be tempting, but what the devil calls glory, God calls vainglory; what the devil calls riches will soon fall away—unlike the treasures in heaven that Jesus urges us to store up for ourselves. (Matthew 6:20)

A trick of the eye

Satan *"showed"* Jesus the power and wealth that he was offering Him. Eve saw that the fruit of the tree of knowledge of good and evil was *"pleasant to the eye,"* and she was unable to resist. The eyes are well suited for conveying temptation. The Apostle John warned of *"a craving for everything we see."* Solomon warned of the consequences of looking at anything that might be an occasion for sin; for example:

Do not gaze at wine when it is red,
when it sparkles in the cup,
when it goes down smoothly!

In the end it bites like a snake
and poisons like a viper.

(Proverbs 23:31–32)

Job, who was described by God as *"blameless and upright, a man who fears God and shuns evil"* (Job 1:8), spoke of his determination to avoid another kind of temptation: *"I made a covenant with my eyes not to look lustfully at a young woman."* (Job 31:1)

There is a story in the book of Joshua that tells of the tragic consequences that may result from being led astray by a look. After the walls of Jericho fell and the men of the Israelite army were about to ravage the city, Joshua gave explicit orders that any silver or gold and any items made of bronze were to be set aside as sacred to the Lord; all such things were to go into the treasury of the Lord's house. The next day, the Israelites attempted to take another city and were defeated in what should have been an easy battle. When Joshua asked the Lord why this had happened— had the Lord decided to desert His people?—God told him that He was displeased because one of the Israelites had stolen some of those things that were supposed to be devoted to Him.

It was finally discovered that a man named Achan was the culprit. In his confession, Achan said, *"When I saw in the plunder a beautiful robe from Babylonia, two hundred shekels of silver and a bar of gold weighing fifty shekels, I coveted them and took them. They are hidden in the ground inside my tent, with the silver underneath."* (Joshua 7:20–21) Achan was probably not a dishonest man; when he headed into Jericho along with his comrades, the theft of sacred objects may have been the farthest thing from his mind. But he *"saw,"* then *"coveted,"* then *"took."* The result was horrific. Everything Achan owned was taken from him: his cattle, donkeys, and sheep, his tent and all that was in it. Then Achan and his sons and daughters—in fact, all the members of his family—were stoned to death, and their bodies were burned. All because of a "look."

When Jesus was up on that mountain, He didn't even glance at the wonders the devil was trying to show Him. He didn't raise a question as to whether Satan had the right to make the offer he was making. He answered, once again, with God's Word: " 'It is written, "Worship the Lord your God, and serve only him." ' " But He also said something else. After all of the devil's challenges, Jesus confronted him directly: " 'Away with you, Satan!' " (Matthew 4:10 NRSV) The result? "Then the devil left him, and suddenly angels came and waited on him." (Matthew 4:11 NRSV)

James tells us that if we follow Jesus' example in times of temptation, we will enjoy the same success: "Resist the devil, and he will flee from you." (James 4:7)

A multiplicity of pitfalls

Being tempted shouldn't come as a surprise to any believer, although a *specific* temptation might come when it is least expected. No Christian is exempt, no matter what level of spiritual maturity or religious office the person has achieved. Consider:

- People who are "doing well," with a beautiful family and good friends, respected in their community, active members of their church. Life is easy for them. They might be in danger of letting down their guard, of failing to "watch and pray."

- People whom God has raised from anonymity and elevated to undreamed–of heights. God has plans for using them, entrusts them with certain tasks, gives them specific instructions. They might be tempted to try doing things their own way or to listen to the suggestions of others, as happened with King Saul.

- People who are "doing right," feeling relaxed, untroubled, enjoying victories over temptations long past. Potential seduction might be waiting just around the corner—or next door, as happened with King David.

- People who are called by God to lead a more consecrated life, perhaps to embark on full–time ministry. They withdraw from the world to meditate and seek God in prayer. They might go through unexpected difficulties that test their faithfulness, as happened with Jesus.

Temptation itself, of course, is not a sin. The sin comes only if the devil is successful in taking advantage of our desires and seducing us into conscious disobedience of God.

Some people seem to think it is God who tempts them. The Bible states categorically, *"No one, when tempted, should say, 'I am being tempted by God'; for God … tempts no one."* (James 1:13 *NRSV)* The neighbor is not the one who tempts us, nor the co-worker. It's not the internet or magazines or television or displays in the shop windows. It's not luxury or beauty. All these things are Satan's advertising department, the instruments he uses in his attempts to deceive us.

The Bible declares, *"Our struggle is not against flesh and blood, but against the rulers, against the authorities, against the powers of this dark world and against the spiritual forces of evil in the heavenly realms."* (Ephesians 6:12) Satan is the one who tempts us. He and his demonic minions do all they can to take advantage of our past; our weaknesses, aspirations, and fears; our emotional, material, and spiritual needs; and every aspect of our personality. They try to put stumbling blocks in our path, create doubt, and motivate disobedience—which brings us condemnation.

The devil is always on the prowl. So we must be always on alert.

A source of strength

Have you ever heard someone say, "If I only had the strength to say no!"? Many people feel that their lives would be completely different if they were able to master their own impulses. Giving in to our passions and desires prevents submission to God and condemns us to unhappiness.

This lack of self-control is essentially spiritual weakness. What is the answer to this problem? Do we need to have our strength increased? The fact is that Satan is so much more powerful than we are that human strength, no matter how great, is never adequate to defeat him. But God speaks this word of encouragement to us: *"The one who is in you is greater than the one who is in the world."* (1 John 4:4)

What we need is not to get stronger, but to tap into *His strength.* The Apostle Paul records that when he asked that his "thorn in the flesh" be taken away from him, the Lord said to him: *"' ... my power is made perfect in weakness.' Therefore I will boast all the more gladly about my weaknesses, so that Christ's power may rest on me. ... For when I am weak, then I am strong."* (2 Corinthians 12:9, 10) The prophet Isaiah declared, *"Those who hope in the Lord will renew their strength."* (Isaiah 40:31) But the word translated "renew" actually means "exchange"; that is, the ones who hope in the Lord will exchange *their* strength for *His*.

No one can withstand temptation without the Lord's help and protection. Ironically, Psalm 91—the very psalm quoted by Satan in his attempt to persuade Jesus to throw Himself down from the Temple tower—contains powerful images representing the protection available to everyone who has sought refuge in God.

> *You who live in the shelter of the Most High, who abide*
> *in the shadow of the Almighty, will say to the Lord, 'My*
> *refuge and my fortress; my God, in whom I trust.' For*
> *he will deliver you from the snare of the fowler and from*
> *the deadly pestilence. (Psalm 91:1–3 NRSV)*

In the midst of the scorching siege of temptations and trials, the believer is invited to enjoy the cool relief and comfort of God's shadow. He is an impenetrable stronghold, an infinitely reliable protector. When the enemy has set his traps and is lurking and ready to pounce, or when the foul, disease–laden pollution of sin threatens to overwhelm the believer, God will deliver.

The Corinthian church was besieged by incitements to all kinds of sin: idolatry, sexual immorality, murmuring, and, in particular, arrogance and spiritual pride. The Apostle Paul was prompted to write:

> *If you think you are standing strong, be careful not to*
> *fall. The temptations in your life are no different from*
> *what others experience. And God is faithful. He will not*
> *allow the temptation to be more than you can stand.*

*When you are tempted, he will also show you a way out
so that you can endure. (1 Corinthians 10:12–13 NLT)*

What about you?

Do you find yourself struggling with temptation? The Lord is *"able to keep you from stumbling."* (Jude 24) He is always willing to help—and waiting to be asked. Actually, temptation will represent a real danger in your life only if you allow sin to gain ground due to neglect of your relationship with your heavenly Father. You cannot continue standing steadfast unless you continue kneeling before God. To ask for help to overcome temptation is to humbly recognize your weaknesses and limitations and admit God's almighty power and grace.

> *Have we trials and temptations?*
> *Is there trouble anywhere?*
> *We should never be discouraged:*
> *Take it to the Lord in prayer.[1]*

Remember that the first words of Jesus' response to each of the devil's temptations were these: *"It is written."* That should give you a clue that, in addition to practicing prayer, the surest way to triumph over temptation is to use the Scriptures. Of course, to use the Scriptures, you have to know the Scriptures.

Jesus used the Word of God to resist Satan, and the tempter quickly ran out of arguments. He retreated, ashamed and defeated. But that didn't mean he wouldn't be back. Luke's account of Jesus' ordeal in the wilderness ends this way: *"When the*

---

1   "What a Friend We Have in Jesus," words by Joseph M. Scriven, 1855.

devil had finished all this tempting, he left him until an opportune time." (Luke 4:13) Satan doesn't give up easily. That's why you must *"Watch and pray so that you will not fall into temptation."* (Matthew 26:41)

Once you have become part of God's kingdom, you and the devil are at war. You are mortal enemies. That's why he tempts you. You must live prepared for battle.

> *Finally, be strong in the Lord and in his mighty power.*
> *Put on the full armor of God, so that you can take your*
> *stand against the devil's schemes. ... Stand firm then,*
> *with the belt of truth buckled around your waist, with*
> *the breastplate of righteousness in place, and with your*
> *feet fitted with the readiness that comes from the gospel of*
> *peace. In addition to all this, take up the shield of faith,*
> *with which you can extinguish all the flaming arrows of*
> *the evil one. Take the helmet of salvation and the sword*
> *of the Spirit, which is the word of God. And pray in*
> *the Spirit on all occasions with all kinds of prayers and*
> *requests.* (Ephesians 6:10–11, 14–18)

Let us pray ...

> Loving and omnipotent God, I come to ask you to protect me from the temptations of this life. Give me the power to be strong, and the wisdom to discern when the enemy is at work. Refresh your Word to my mind so that I may resist the devil and put him to flight. Be my shelter, O Lord. Wrap me in your wings. You are my refuge, and I will wait before you. I ask these things in Jesus' name.
>
> Amen

11

"Deliver us from evil"

Rely on your Father's protection

THE WORLD IS FULL OF threats to the human race. As a result, millions of people spend their entire lives filled with fear. They are afraid of financial ruin, of terrorist attacks, of global warming, of infectious diseases, of divorce, of loneliness, of being discredited and slandered, of vandalism, of death, and of the unknown. Although many fears are unfounded, many real dangers exist and cannot be ignored. But is it right to call all these things evil?

The Scriptures have a great deal to say on this subject. The word "evil" and other terms that are virtual synonyms appear 1,107 times in the Bible,[1] in 33 of the 39 books of the Old Testament and in 26 of the 27 books of the New Testament. It is important to understand that in many cases, these words do not refer to *intent*, but strictly to *effect*. That is, "evil" does not always mean "wickedness."

What is evil? It is anything that is *harmful in its influence or impact*, whether physical, emotional, moral, or spiritual. Some evils attack the body. Some evils attack the emotions and the

---

1   According to *Zondervan NIV Exhaustive Concordance* (Zondervan, 1999).

spirit. There are evils that weaken our sanity and evils that undermine our relationships with others. And there are evils that harm the environment, both local and worldwide.

What is the source of evil? Satan is the ultimate cause of all evil. In fact, nearly all modern translations of the New Testament render this line from Jesus' teaching on prayer as follows: "Deliver us from the evil *one*" (Matthew 6:13). When Eve and Adam made the choice to obey the devil instead of God, the curse of evil descended on the world. The perfect, life–sustaining Garden of Eden, which should have been the dwelling place of humanity for all time, was now closed off. The earth, the dwelling place for Adam and Eve and all their descendants, was cursed. And human life, which God had intended to be never–ending, now faced the inevitable destiny of death.

Satan had won the battle and claimed his place as the prince of this world. His intention was—and is—to spread universal evil. From that reality spring all the ills that affect creation: natural disasters, accidents, illness, criminal acts and every kind of sin, and, ultimately, death itself.

Satan's power to do evil

We should never underestimate our enemy's great power to do evil. However, neither should we exaggerate his abilities or think that he can do whatever he pleases. Someone has said that the devil is a roaring lion on which God has tied a rope, so that he can move only a limited distance. He has power to harm, but God, who created him, set limits to his actions and can undo his work. When our heavenly Father says "Enough!" the devil must stop. God sets limits for Satan, hinders his plans, and sends angels to oppose him, especially in support of those who have claimed Him as their refuge and hope.

Some people think that one of the limits on the devil's power is the believer's immunity to most of the world's troubles. Since the middle years of the 20th century, false prophets have arisen in the Church teaching what the Apostle Paul would call *"a different gospel"* (2 Corinthians 11:4)—one according to which the children of God are entitled to material prosperity and a life of endless miracles, including freedom from injury or disease. Many people who have accepted this teaching eventually come to the conclusion—because they are not experiencing this "divine health and divine wealth"—that they have sinned in some way or that they just don't have enough faith to please God. They become confused, discouraged, frustrated, and resentful, and some have even been known to return to the world.

The Gospel preached by the Apostle Paul and by the Church through the ages certainly teaches that God heals and delivers and provides for every need. On the other hand, Jesus gave His disciples a warning that also applies to us: *"In this world you will have trouble."* (John 16:33)

Sadly, for some believers, that warning from Jesus virtually becomes a "life Scripture verse." They labor under a delusion that God has destined them to a life of suffering and that they must resign themselves to their fate. With each tragic situation, they are quick to say, "It's God's will, so I have to accept it." "I resign myself to whatever God sends my way."

In many cases, a better first response might be: "Do I bear any responsibility for what is happening to me?"

Satan delights in seeing human beings suffer evil. And he delights even more when he can persuade them to act in such a way as to create evil, to make themselves and others suffer.

Satan's deceptiveness

Day and night, Satan is active in his quest to extend his influence in the world. Where he is in danger of losing ground because of the preaching of the Gospel and the advancement of God's kingdom, he concentrates his efforts on deception. He is *a liar and the father of lies"* (John 8:44). He works tirelessly to keep people from coming to a knowledge of God's truth. The Apostle Paul called Satan *"the god of this age"* who *"has blinded the minds of unbelievers, so that they cannot see the light of the gospel."* (2 Corinthians 4:4) And of course, the devil is always busy trying to confound minds and manipulate the truth.

Isaiah warns:

> *Woe to those who call evil good and good evil,*
> *who put darkness for light and light for darkness,*
> *who put bitter for sweet and sweet for bitter.*

(Isaiah 5:20)

When values are twisted, evil consequences will follow. Many societies now accept—and even acclaim—as normal and appropriate behaviors and practices that both the Bible and natural reason condemn. Among these practices are sexual union between people of the same gender and between people who are not married; utter dishonesty in the business world, the political world, and everyday life; and disdain and hatred toward those who are "different" in color, ethnicity, national origin, language, or religious beliefs. What "contemporary wisdom" considers normal, God calls sin.

Of course, it should be out of the question that any Christian would condone such practices, let alone engage in them. The cultural pressures to conform may be very powerful; but in defining *"Religion that God our Father accepts as pure and faultless,"* James included these words: *" ... to keep oneself from being polluted by the world."* (James 1:27)

Yet Satan's deceitfulness may cause us to fall prey to less obvious transgressions that are equally sinful and equally destructive. An example is being ungrateful. The Bible says, *"Evil will never leave the house of one who pays back evil for good."* (Proverbs 17:13) Ingratitude is a selfish attitude and action that closes doors; it separates friends and generates resentment. Many people can't find anyone who will help them in time of need because they have been ungrateful in the past. They end up saying that God has abandoned them, when the truth is that they are reaping what they have sown.

Speaking of His unfaithful and ungrateful people, God says, *"They sow the wind, and they shall reap the whirlwind."* (Hosea 8:7 *NRSV*) Just so, what we think, speak, do, and wish for can yield a harvest of evil, far beyond what we could have imagined.

We need to pray, *"Deliver us from evil."* But if we expect God to deliver us from succumbing to the grasp of the evil one, we must first obey His Word. *"The Lord's angel camps around <u>the Lord's loyal followers</u> and delivers them."* (Psalm 34:7 *NET*)

Human folly

Have you heard the story of how the devil, tired of being blamed for all the troubles of the world, sat down by the side of the road and started to cry? A Christian who was passing by saw him and asked what was wrong. The devil said, "Everyone blames me for every bad thing that happens. I'm sick and tired of it." The Christian, in an effort to provide comfort, put his hand on Satan's shoulder and said: "Don't listen to what people say. That's of the devil."

Any believer who constantly feels blameworthy has in fact been taken in by the devil's lies. Satan is *"the accuser of our brothers and sisters"* (Revelation 12:10). His desire is that we spend our lives regretting all the wrong things we have done, when what we need to do is confess those sins to the Father, receive forgiveness for them, and leave them behind. The devil also wants, if at all possible, to make us feel guilty for many evils that are not our fault. If you hear a persistent voice in your head telling you how bad you are, you can be sure that's Satan's voice.

On the other hand, even though the devil really is to blame for all the ills of the world, that doesn't let human beings—even believers—off the hook. The evil one takes advantage of our weaknesses, and many afflictions and calamities result from our own actions. Sinful actions have consequences, not only in the age to come, but also in this life. And sometimes the problem is not sin as such, but thoughtless, poor decision-making:

- *"Those who trust in themselves are fools."* (Proverbs 28:26)

- *"Fools die for lack of sense."* (Proverbs 10:21)

None of us likes to be called a fool. But when we look at the consequences of decisions we have made and things we have done—or failed to do—we may recognize that the label is sometimes not an inappropriate one.

It's natural to want to dodge our responsibility and simply blame the devil for everything bad that happens to us. But in many cases what Satan does is take advantage of a situation we ourselves have created to cause us grief. Therefore, whenever we encounter trouble, we should examine ourselves in light of God's Word and our own reasoning to see whether what is affecting us may be a result of action or omission on our part.

Each day, doctors treat millions of patients suffering from diseases or injuries that are the result of abuse or neglect of the body. I have known people who have developed severe illnesses, and in some cases died, as a result of excess in eating and drinking.

I met Julio in 1981, when we were both working for an oil company. He was relatively young, and a department manager; his future was bright. Julio began to experience some discomfort, so he went to see his doctor. After several tests, the doctor told him he was at risk for diabetes and that he had to watch his diet in addition to undergoing some treatment. For a few days, Julio followed his doctor's advice; but as soon as he felt better, he returned to his old habits, eating and drinking whatever he wanted. As a result, his health deteriorated. At one point, he went into a diabetic coma, from which he made a difficult recovery. After that, even though his health continued to fail, Julio did not stop drinking beer. He went blind, and finally died.

Many people who knew Julio said, "God took him"; but he was no different from millions of others who suffer from illnesses resulting from abuse of alcohol, cigarettes, drugs (including prescription drugs), or steroids; from consumption of foods with high levels of fats and carbohydrates; and from irresponsible sexual practices. The list of ensuing consequences includes addiction, obesity, heart disease, kidney disease, cancer, neurological impairment—a wide variety of serious illnesses and disabilities. These in turn can lead to financial failure, family conflicts, depression, and suicide—all on account of self-indulgence.

Human carelessness

Carelessness and recklessness can also cause evils that are debilitating, and even horrific, in their effects. Proverbs says, *"A prudent person foresees danger and takes precautions. The simpleton goes blindly on and suffers the consequences."* (Proverbs 22:3 *NLT*) Some evils come because even though we are aware of the risks, we allow a dangerous situation to continue. Every few months, there is a news report of a child who has shot and killed a playmate with a loaded gun that had been carelessly left within reach. Every summer, there is one case after another of a young child becoming overheated and dying after being left by a parent in a car with the windows shut. It's easier to say, "God needed another angel in heaven" than to admit that the tragedy was caused by carelessness or neglect.

Many parents are unaware of their children's friendships. They don't monitor what their children watch on TV or the internet, the video games they play, or what they read and see—or may themselves write and create—on social media. How, then, can they be surprised if their children get into trouble? In the same vein, many marriages break up as a result of neglect: of respect, care, communication, or intimacy and romance.

If you have a garden and you want it to look beautiful, you have to take care of it. The same rule applies to family relationships. If you stop watering your garden, everything will wither; if you cease to be loving, understanding, fair, patient, respectful, or honest, every member of the family will feel neglected. If you don't remove the weeds in your garden, they will soon spread everywhere; if you allow misunderstandings between husband and wife to fester, you will soon find that you are facing a marital crisis. If you pass over ant hills and do not exterminate them, they will take over more and more territory. If you leave problem issues in your children's lives to be resolved "sometime," or assume they will be addressed by your spouse—or if you bring your problems home from work and take your frustrations out on other members of your family—before you know it, your home will be transformed into an angry, contentious place.

Often, when beauty disappears from the home, the people living there are taken by surprise. They don't understand what has happened; they don't realize that the root cause is neglect.

God's wrath

God has no association with evil. It is utterly abhorrent to Him. *"Far be it from God to do evil, from the Almighty to do wrong."* (Job 34:10) Yet God sends calamities upon the earth, not as a work of evil, but as an act of justice.

The Bible tells of a number of times when God poured out His wrath upon the earth. The first of these accompanied the expulsion of Adam and Eve from Eden and took the form of a curse upon the land. Then, as the human race multiplied in number, people devoted themselves to all kinds of wickedness; in response, God unleashed a flood that inundated the world. God rained down burning sulfur on Sodom and Gomorrah after He was unable to find 10 righteous people in the two cities combined. When the Pharaoh refused to release God's people, the Israelites, from bondage, God poured out horrendous disaster upon the land of Egypt.

After God delivered His people from slavery in Egypt, He

made a covenant with them. It included assurances of great blessing if they obeyed Him and warnings of terrible curses if they did not. As long as they kept His commandments—the first and most important of which was to worship Him alone and not give their allegiance to the idols of other nations—God kept His promises and prospered them in every way. Their land was so fruitful that they could go a year without cultivating it and live on what it produced by itself. They enjoyed the respect of their neighbors, who did not dare cross their borders to attack.

Then the people of Israel began to break their covenant with God; they did this again and again until they had exhausted His patience. God sent His prophets to warn them of the consequences of their disobedience, but most of the people ignored or mocked their messages. Finally God pronounced judgment on them:

> 'People of Israel,' declares the Lord, 'I am bringing a distant nation against you—an ancient and enduring nation, a people whose language you do not know, whose speech you do not understand. ... They will devour your harvests and food, devour your sons and daughters; they will devour your flocks and herds, devour your vines and fig trees. With the sword they will destroy the fortified cities in which you trust. ... And when the people ask, "Why has the Lord our God done all this to us?" you will tell them, "As you have forsaken me and served foreign gods in your own land, so now you will serve foreigners in a land not your own." ' (Jeremiah 5:15, 17, 19)

Just a few hundred years after the Israelites left Egypt for the land God had promised them, many of their descendants—now a divided nation—went into exile. The people of the northern section were taken to Assyria, the people of the south, to Babylon. The kingdom of Israel was never reunited.

The world has not seen the last of God's wrath. Jesus spoke of how it was in *"the days of Noah,"* when *"people were eating and drinking, marrying and giving in marriage, up to the day Noah entered the ark; and they knew nothing about what would happen until the flood came and took them all away."* (Matthew 24:37, 38–39) Jesus said it will be like that in the last days; people will be taken up with the occupations and distractions of life, having fun, involved in all kinds of pleasure, making plans for the future, totally heedless of God ... and suddenly the end will come.

The Apostle Paul wrote, *"We will all stand before God's judgment seat. ... each of us will give an account of ourselves before God."* (Romans 14:10, 12) In that day, people who have never called upon God will call to the mountains and the rocks, *"Fall on us and hide us from the face of him who sits on the throne and from the wrath of the Lamb! For the great day of their wrath has come, and who can withstand it?"* (Revelation 6:16–17) The earth itself will be destroyed (2 Peter 3:10); but in its place will be *"a new heaven and a new earth, where righteousness dwells."* (2 Peter 3:13)

God's victory over Satan

In the biblical accounts of the lives of Noah and Abraham, we see that even when God executed His judgments, He delivered His children from evil. When He sent the flood in reaction to widespread human corruption, He preserved Noah—*"a righteous man, blameless among the people of his time"* (Genesis 6:9)—and his family. When He destroyed Sodom and Gomorrah, He gave the family of Abraham, His friend (Isaiah 41:8), the opportunity to escape. *"The gracious hand of our God is on everyone who looks to him,"* even when *"his great anger is against all who forsake him."* (Ezra 8:22)

The desire of our heavenly Father is to bless and prosper His children and deliver them from evil, whatever its origin. When we obey God, the evil one cannot prevail against us, because our Father does not allow it. We may be under siege, as a city is besieged by an enemy army, but that siege will not be effective, because our God will defend us and fight for us. He promises, *"No weapon that is used against you will defeat you."* (Isaiah 54:17 NCV)

When Jesus told Peter that Satan was going to attack him, He also comforted him with these words: *"I have prayed for you that your own faith may not fail."* (Luke 22:32 NRSV) We can take that promise for our own; when evil confronts us, the intercession of our Savior sustains us.

We will sometimes fight spiritual battles that seem to be beyond our strength and threaten to overwhelm us. There will be satanic attacks designed to weaken our faith, to get us away from God, to have us deny our Savior and finally be lost for eternity. But we must not lose heart. The devil is a defeated foe; Jesus is the victor who vanquished him.

God says:

> *'All who rage against you will surely be ashamed and disgraced; those who oppose you will be as nothing and perish. Though you search for your enemies, you will not find them. Those who wage war against you will be as nothing at all. For I am the Lord your God who takes*

hold of your right hand and says to you, Do not fear; I will help you.'

(Isaiah 41:11–13)

God's protection and deliverance

At no point does God assure us that we will never find ourselves in dire situations. Believers around the world face such natural phenomena as tornadoes and hurricanes, floods, earthquakes, fires, drought, famine, and lack of clean water. We may also experience other events, equally dangerous, that involve some element of human causation: epidemics; acts of violence, domestic and international, on a vast scale or local; accidents of various kinds; and injustice.

God may even allow us to suffer the effects of such calamities right along with those who do not fear Him. But we have His word that if we live under His shelter and depend completely on His protection, we will share in His ultimate victory. When Jesus said, *"In this world you will have trouble,"* He went on to say, *"But take heart! I have overcome the world."* (John 16:33)

The Apostle Paul suffered many things while doing his missionary work. But he also wrote, *"Yet the Lord rescued me from all of them."* (2 Timothy 3:11)

The Bible is full of testimonies to the way God delivered His people in times of trouble: He provided victory in battles and food amid famine; rescue from wild beasts, fiery furnaces, shipwrecks, and prisons; and courage and strength in the face of severe beatings, torture, and martyrdom. (Read Hebrews 11:32–38 and 2 Corinthians 11:23–27.)

And our Father's wonderful care for His children didn't cease with the last pages of the Bible. Through the centuries, God has continued His ministry of deliverance from calamities and works of the devil. The thrilling accounts of wonders and miracles of deliverance told in Scripture and in Christian history stand as monuments, set up to remind us that God has always kept His promises and will always do so.

That truth is the basis for this grand declaration of faith:

> *Who shall separate us from the love of Christ? Shall trouble or hardship or persecution or famine or nakedness or danger or sword? ... No, in all these things we are more than conquerors through him who loved us. For I am convinced that neither death nor life, neither angels nor demons, neither the present nor the future, nor any powers, neither height nor depth, nor anything else in all creation, will be able to separate us from the love of God that is in Christ Jesus our Lord.*
>
> (Romans 8:35, 37–39)

The time will come for the complete eradication of evil. That will take place when the kingdom of God is fully established. On that day, the wicked one will be given his final sentence and be thrown into his eternal prison, the lake of fire. But our Father will comfort His children. *"He will wipe every tear from their eyes. There will be no more death or mourning or crying or pain, for the old order of things has passed away."* (Revelation 21:4) After these words were proclaimed from God's heavenly throne, the Lord said to the Apostle John: *"Write this down, for these words are trustworthy and true."* (Revelation 21:5)

Until that day comes, we pray to our Father to deliver us from evil. *"He has said, 'I will never leave you or forsake you.' So we can say with confidence, 'The Lord is my helper; I will not be afraid. What can anyone do to me?'"* (Hebrews 13:5–6 *NRSV*)

What about you?

Are you facing an impossible situation? Is your strength depleted? Do you feel like there is no way out? Why don't you put everything in God's hands?

When you first come to the Lord, *"Deliver me from evil"* is not a simple request to be rescued from the dangers of this world. It means "Deliver me from bondage to Satan, the evil *one.*" After that, your continuing prayer should be a request to be kept free from sin, to prevent the devil from making any inroads into your life. Your heavenly Father delights to answer this prayer; and you will be able to say with assurance, *"The Lord will rescue me from every evil attack and will bring me safely to his heavenly kingdom."* (2 Timothy 4:18)

Being God's child also means that *"Deliver me from evil"* takes on a whole new meaning. You are qualified to ask your Father to protect you from the multitude of dangers in this world. He promises deliverance to those who love Him. He says:

> *Those who love me, I will deliver; I will protect those who know my name. When they call to me, I will answer them; I will be with them in trouble, I will rescue them and honor them. With long life I will satisfy them, and show them my salvation.*

> (Psalm 91:14–16 *NRSV*)

Let us pray...

Heavenly Father, you know my weaknesses and you
know that I sometimes face dangers that are beyond
my strength. The enemy is always on the prowl, seeking every opportunity to try to hurt me and lead me
away from you. So I ask you to protect me from the
evil one. Also help me to be wise and recognize things
I might do that could hurt me or others; deliver
me from my own mistakes. Shelter me under your
shadow and sustain me by your power. Help me to
hold firmly to you, so that your name may be glorified in me. I pray in the name of Jesus.

Amen

12

"For yours is the kingdom and the power and the glory forever"

Acknowledge the truth about God

"IF YOU WANT TO KNOW who dies in *Harry Potter*, the answer is easy: God. Harry Potter lives in a world free of religion or spirituality of any kind. He lives surrounded by ghosts but has no one to pray to, even if he were so inclined, which he isn't." This striking statement appeared in an article by Lev Grossman in the issue of *TIME* magazine dated July 23, 2007. *(Harry Potter,* of course, is a series of fantasy novels by J.K. Rowling; the series has enjoyed enormous popularity worldwide, and several of the books were turned into movies.) Grossman added that we are living in a millennium in which "psychology and technology have superseded the sacred."

It is not surprising that an atheistic philosophy should underlie popular literature and other forms of modern communication. To a large proportion of people in the Western world, God is an invention created by ignorant human beings to make sense of what they don't understand. Supposedly, there is no need for such constructs in 21st–century thinking.

The fact is, however, that in every human heart there is a need, and a longing, for God. Witness the advent of a podcast called "Harry Potter and the Sacred Text," described in an article in the "Acts of Faith" section of *The Washington Post* for July 19, 2017. A large number of Americans who consider themselves "spiritual but not religious" say that the magic and mythology of the Harry Potter books—along with the ethical themes they find in each chapter—provide them with spiritual sustenance. The article reported that hundreds of podcast fans across the country were meeting in reading groups—"akin to Bible study more than book club." In addition, two divinity school graduates were hosting "a weekly church–like service" in Harvard Square in Cambridge, Massachusetts, focusing on a Harry Potter text.

Whether people reject the notion of God altogether or seek Him in the religions of the world—or in a Harry Potter podcast—there is a set of unshakable truths about Him. And the Apostle Paul said that for anyone to claim complete ignorance of God is inexcusable:

> *For what can be known about God is plain to them, because God has shown it to them. Ever since the creation of the world his eternal power and divine nature, invisible though they are, have been understood and seen through the things he has made. (Romans 1:19–20 NRSV)*

Creation provides clear evidence of its Creator, and we who know Him have an additional foundation, even more firm, for what we know about Him: God's Word, on which we base our faith. *"By faith we understand that the entire universe was formed at God's command, that what we now see did not come from anything that can be seen."* (Hebrews 11:3 *NLT*) For us, the universe of which we are a part is corroborating visible testimony to God's greatness, power, and glory.

The God to whom we pray

It is impossible for human beings to begin to conceive the scope of God's power and authority or even to imagine His eternal existence. What we do know about Him is only what He has revealed to us. But that knowledge is of vital importance, particularly when we pray. We must know and believe the truths that the Bible proclaims about God. Without those truths, the whole basis of our faith and the hope of millions of believers who lived before us crumbles, and we are to be pitied. But God's Word is true. And when our faith is utterly centered on God's revelation of Himself, we have access through prayer to His unlimited capabilities.

"The kingdom and the power and the glory" belong to God—*"forever."* This declaration at the end of the model for prayer offered by Jesus establishes three pillars that support the ability of God to answer the prayers of His children.

Some renowned scholars in the study of Gospel manuscripts have pointed out that this doxology—which appears in some translations—was not included in the most ancient texts. However, the authority for the declaration is also affirmed elsewhere in Scripture:

> *Yours, Lord, is the greatness and the power and the*
> *glory and the majesty and the splendor, for everything in*
> *heaven and earth is yours. Yours, Lord, is the kingdom;*
> *you are exalted as head over all. (1 Chronicles 29:11)*

In the first chapter of this book, I offered the following definition of prayer:

> Prayer is a testimony of dependence and an act of surrender to a Being who is infinitely greater than ourselves. It is a way of exalting that Being and recognizing His nature, His attributes, and His ability to meet all our needs; a way to sustain our hope, dispel our fears, and reaffirm, while living in this world, the values on which our faith is founded.

When we confess the final part of the Lord's Prayer, we are proclaiming God's sovereignty, His authority to govern and maintain His kingdom, and the honor that belongs only to Him as the Creator and Savior of humanity. Our first purpose in prayer is to worship and revere Him.

The conjunction *for* at the beginning of this final line of the prayer affirms that all the preceding requests can be answered and satisfied because—*for*—God has all the resources required for that purpose. Each *for* that follows is a testimony to the sufficiency of God to meet all our needs.

"For yours is the kingdom ... forever"

The first *for* that ensures that God can help us is that *"the kingdom"* is His. God's kingdom:

- Is unlimited in extent. *"The Lord has established his throne in heaven, and his kingdom rules over all.* (Psalm 103:19)

- Is light in a dark world. *"... the Father ... has qualified you to share in the inheritance of his holy people in the kingdom of light."* (Colossians 1:12)

- Is active. *"The kingdom of God is not a matter of talk but of power."* (1 Corinthians 4:20)

- Is immovable. *"Since we are receiving a kingdom that cannot be shaken, let us be thankful, and so worship God acceptably with reverence and awe."* (Hebrews 12:28)

- Is eternal. *"Your kingdom is an everlasting kingdom."* (Psalm 145:13)

Our heavenly Father is in control and remains the supreme universal authority. The psalmist proclaims His sovereignty in absolute terms:

> *The Lord reigns, let the nations tremble; he sits enthroned between the cherubim, let the earth shake. Great is the Lord in Zion; he is exalted over all the nations. Let them praise your great and awesome name. (Psalm 99:1–3)*

In heaven, the cherubim represent the highest echelon of angels, and God reigns over them. On earth, His presence shakes the planet's very foundations and all peoples are subject to His will.

When we pray, we must remember that God has total, categorical authority—to rule, to ban, to suppress, or to allow. He is not subject to anyone, depends on no one, and does not ask permission. When He is determined to carry out a purpose, nothing in the universe can stop Him. He is above all limitations, all heavenly and earthly powers. With respect to humankind, He dominates the material and the spiritual, life and death, the present and the future.

To declare *"yours is the kingdom"* is to recognize God's government. It may seem at times as if evil were acting without restraint. But God has set a day when every power in heaven and on earth will confess His authority *"… and he will reign for ever and ever."* (Revelation 11:15)

"For yours is the power … forever"

The second *for* is that *"the power"* belongs to our heavenly Father. King David wrote it just that simply: *"Power belongs to you, God."* (Psalm 62:11)

God is omnipotent, meaning "all–powerful." He is able to do what is impossible for human beings or for angels. When we pray, we must believe, declare, and expect that God is able to respond and act on our behalf. At the dedication of the Temple in Jerusalem, King Solomon said to the gathered assembly, *"Praise be to the Lord, the God of Israel, who with his hands has fulfilled what he promised with his mouth to my father David."* (2 Chronicles 6:4) God has promised many wonderful things in His Word, and He can and will make good on His promises.

When thinking about God's power, it is helpful for us to keep in mind that prior to him there was no other; so God is the original source of all power. No entity in heaven or earth can possibly be more powerful than He is. Consider:

> *The Lord sends death, and he brings to life. He sends people to the grave, and he raises them to life again. The Lord makes some people poor, and others he makes rich. He makes some people humble, and others he makes great. The Lord raises the poor up from the dust, and he*

lifts the needy from the ashes. He lets the poor sit with princes and receive a throne of honor. (1 Samuel 2:6–8 NCV)

To know that God is in control of all things should fill us with confidence and joy. When we pray according to our Father's will, all the resources in His storehouse will be brought to bear on our case. *"This is the confidence we have in approaching God: that if we ask anything according to his will, he hears us. And if we know that he hears us—whatever we ask—we know that we have what we asked of him."* (1 John 5:14–15)

We can live victorious over our worries and cares if we believe that God has the power to ensure the provision of our daily bread, to keep us from temptation, to deliver us from evil, and more.

"For yours is the glory … forever"

The third *for* is that *"the glory"* belongs to our heavenly Father. "Glory" is a word for the absolute excellence of God, the perfection that sets Him apart from all created things, including human beings. He has declared that He will not share His glory with anyone or anything else. (Isaiah 42:8)

In Ephesians 1:17, Paul refers to God as *"the Father of glory" (NRSV)*. His essence is characterized by splendor and magnificence. James calls Him *"the Father of lights"* (James 1:17 NRSV), the source of all light. The light of the glory of God is on display in the created universe. *"The heavens declare the glory of God; the skies proclaim the work of his hands."* (Psalm 19:1)

James 1:17 also says that *"the Father of lights"* is the source of every good gift we receive. When our prayers are answered, we should not neglect to recognize that our glorious Father is the

One who is blessing us; He must receive thanks and praise and honor. We would never want to deny God the glory He deserves. Every prayer that fails to acknowledge God's glory is a demonstration of arrogance. *"The Lord Almighty—he is the King of glory."* (Psalm 24:10)

Humans can be honored for any number of qualities or skills or accomplishments. However, God is the *giver* of all talents: artistic, intellectual, scientific, athletic, technological, and financial. Any distinction attained by a human being is nothing when compared to who God is and what He does. God has not received His excellence from anyone; it is part of His divine identity. So He must be praised above all others.

Scripture does not hold back on expressions of praise to God. We are exhorted to join in:

> *Oh, sing to the Lord a new song!*
> *Sing to the Lord, all the earth.*
> *Sing to the Lord, bless His name …*
> *For the Lord is great and greatly to be praised …*
> *Honor and majesty are before Him;*
> *Strength and beauty are in His sanctuary. …*
> *Give to the Lord the glory due His name;*
> *Bring an offering, and come into His courts.*
> *Oh, worship the Lord in the beauty of holiness!*
> *Tremble before Him, all the earth.*
>
> (Psalm 96:1–2, 4, 6, 7–8 *NKJV*)

Before such magnificence, all earthly glory pales into insignificance. So the Apostle Paul, writing to Timothy, his son in the faith, poured out his soul in worship and praise: *"Now to the King eternal, immortal, invisible, the only God, be honor and glory for ever and ever. Amen."* (1 Timothy 1:17)

What about you?

If you have read this far in this book, no doubt it is because you have felt the same concerns that motivated those early disciples of Jesus who, impelled by their inner need, said to him, "Lord, teach us to pray." My hope and prayer is that the Holy Spirit has used these reflections to help you in your Christian growth.

Prayer is not an option; it is a vital discipline for every believer. The goal of every child of God should be to get the greatest edification from it and, in the process, to bring joy to His heart. Every one of us who is a disciple of Jesus would do well to pay attention to His teachings. Then we can say, as He did: *"Father, I thank You that You have heard me. And I know that you always hear me."* (John 11:41–42 *NKJV*)

Let us pray...

> Now to him who is able to do immeasurably more than all we ask or imagine, according to his power that is at work within us, to him be glory in the church and in Christ Jesus throughout all generations, for ever and ever! (Ephesians 3:20–21)